MW00943949

GOD

INSIDE THE FIRE

An Amazing True Story

GREG STELLEY

ISBN# *978-1477499917*

CONTENTS

INTRODUCTION

I. THE CEDAR FIRE

II. GOD AND FIRE

For Joni
Faith and belief do not describe your relationship with God.
Two words do — God is.

INTRODUCTION

Every fireman has a secret. He holds it close, he never speaks of it, but he knows it to be true. He has seen them too often to even doubt anymore, but then, what would his buddies think? So he keeps quiet about it. When asked, a fireman will shrug his shoulders and say: "Strange things happen in a fire." But a fireman knows better. His spirit whispers truths to him that never pass his lips... *There are miracles during wildfires.*

I am not a fireman, but I know the fireman's secret. What follows is my attempt to share a life-changing occurrence with you. A supernatural occurrence that I experienced firsthand. Even to this day I am shocked and amazed at what I witnessed in the fall of 2003.

Of course, before the miracle, there was the fire...

I was first introduced to the awesome power of uncontrollable fire one early summer evening in 1961. I was four years old and ready for bed in my Superman pajamas when my father received a call from Uncle Gene, whose family lived a mile from us on higher ground in Lemon Grove, a small town seven miles east of San Diego. He told my father that he could see a huge fire below, which could only mean one building—the massive, three-story, fruit packing plant. Built in the 1920s and made entirely of wood, it was a firetrap in search of a fire. It found one that night. Within seconds, Dad hurried Mom, my younger sister and me into the station wagon and we drove toward the inferno to take a closer look. This was before color television or "Eye in the Sky" helicopters. In those days, when disaster struck, the whole town showed up. I remember standing with my little sister and three older female cousins in a huge crowd of children, all of us in pajamas, while massive flames rolled to the starry sky.

I stared through a gaping hole in the wall of the fully engulfed building, amazed by the intense color and bizarre realities inside the fire. It seemed to my young mind that the burning building had a secret world inside it, a sparkling and alien planet that you could view but never visit, a place where nothing could survive. It was surreal. It was hypnotic. And it was *hot*. I could feel the heat through my pajamas though we stood behind fire lines more than two hundred feet from the spectacular flames. Dozens of firemen near a line of red pumper trucks sprayed thousands of gallons of water on the raging building while circling lights flashed on faces in the crowd, but nothing could stop that fire. I remember finding some of my little pals from the neighborhood. We pointed and screamed as the third floor collapsed onto the second, causing the whole building to burst into white-hot flames in a thunder clap explosion and a swarm of firefly sparks. The show was over, but the secret world within fire has continued on in my memory for all these years.

As it happened, my career as an adult provided a scientific understanding of what fire *is*. I completed gas technician school in 1998 through the utility company for which I work. I learned how fire functions—how it lives, how it breathes, and how it dies. By October 2003, I was settled into my vocation after five years of hourly experiences with controlled flame. I felt very confident in my understanding of flame characteristics, but since that fiery night long ago in 1961, I've never forgotten the terrible truth about fire. *Sometimes it gets out.*

Just before sunset on Saturday, October 25th, 2003, in mountains sixty miles to the northeast of the city of San Diego, a lost hunter set a signal fire during a raging eastern wind. This seemingly innocent act—a cry for help that began as a single spark—would quickly become a catastrophic event of historical significance. That signal fire rapidly became the largest firestorm in the history of California.

Carried along on strong Santa Ana winds, what became known as the Cedar Fire traveled southwest at the speed of a galloping horse. Between midnight and three in the morning, it mushroomed from 5,500 to 62,000 acres, expanding eleven times in size. Hundreds of people in the onrushing path of the rampaging firestorm were jolted awake around 3:00 a.m. by hot choking smoke. Bleary-eyed and confused, they fled their burning homes wearing only bedclothes. Panicked and frightened, they dashed through scorching flames, stumbled into their cars, then lurched their burning vehicles forward, careening blindly down the flaming gauntlet road. Some drove through one-hundred-foot-high walls of flame to try to make it out alive.

Tires melted. Engines stalled. Fuel tanks exploded. People died. Thirteen burned to death that first night. The next morning their grisly remains were found still clutching their steering wheels.

When the Cedar Fire was finally contained ten days later it had blackened a staggering total of 273,246 acres or an incredible 427 square miles. The flames destroyed 2,232 homes and killed a total of 15 people, one of whom was a fireman. Entire towns were incinerated.

On November 3, 2003, President Bush flew in on Air Force One to view the colossal damage. He surveyed several destroyed neighborhoods within the charcoaled center of San Diego County, a 30-mile-wide swath of black. Later, the President got out and walked through the destroyed rural hamlet of Crest. He personally consoled hundreds of homeowners who had lost everything.

"We've seen the worst of nature... but the absolute best of mankind," said the President.

The Los Angeles Times called the Cedar Fire: "the state's worst wildfire in 75 years..."

CNN described it as: "perhaps the state's most devastating..."

New York Times reporter Nick Madigan may have described it best: "conditions are little short of hellish..."

Colin Wilson, a 20-year veteran fire chief from a Northern California fire department, wrote an account of his experience with the Cedar Fire, his first battle with a magnitude 10 firestorm.

"In the course of our various assignments we were exposed to fire at a level that was totally new to all of us. In one conversation we agreed that we saw more and bigger fire in two days than all of us had seen collectively in our entire careers... On at least one occasion we survived by dumb luck and the grace of God... Cuyamaca is a small town built around a lake that is about two miles long and one mile wide. A high ring of peaks surrounds the community to the north, west and south. To the east, the valley runs out into an old dry lake bed which is the direction we entered from. As we approached the town from the east, we saw an incredible column of smoke rising from the high ridge to the west. It stretched from north to south as far as we could see, rising straight up as a solid wall that appeared to have no end."

Echoing *New York Times* reporter Nick Madigan, Wilson found a scene that inspired a dramatic description. But his assessment was simply accurate.

"I am not at all a religious person but as we drove in and looked at the approaching fire and smoke column the only words that came to mind tended to be biblical in nature: holocaust, jihad, apocalyptic. In truth, I don't have words in my vocabulary that would express the massive, raw, unrestrained force that was about to descend on the town. In my nearly 20 years in the fire service, I have never felt as threatened and afraid as I did that afternoon. In my heart I was saying to myself, 'What are we doing driving into this?"

The last six cataclysmic days of October 2003, brought human tragedies in greater number than any firestorm in San Diego's history.

Thousands of firefighters drove into the enormous and terrifying inferno to defend what they could, while legions of horrified homeowners fled for their lives. Their selfless acts of courage saved the homes of thousands of strangers the firemen would never meet. This rare and special dedication was reflected back to the firemen in the admiration and heartfelt gratitude of millions. It leaves us asking — where does such a powerful and magnanimous motivation come from? What is its source? It is as if this zealous devotion was there all the time, waiting just behind the world's curtain. After earthquakes or hurricanes it is this selfless type of love that brings the rescuers, surgeons and engineers to the victims of disaster, ready to help, eager to serve and desperate to save.

If you and I were allowed to see beyond the physical world, to step behind whatever curtain partitions us from the unseen, what would we see? Utter darkness? Marvelous light? Malevolent hatred? Benevolent love? Both? After all, looters, thieves and frauds prey upon the same victims the rescuers work to save. Who or what motivates such conspicuous evil? Such unequivocal good? These diametrically opposed impulses are both larger than our ability to fully comprehend, yet we know they exist.

An extraordinary event occurred right in the heart of the Cedar Fire. It involved two families. My family, my wife, Joni, and my children, Danielle, 9 and Juliette, 8 at the time, and our dear friends, the Scalari family, Frank and Kathy and their four children, Frankie, Veronica, Alex and Anna, ages 16, 13, 9 and 5. Our children played together, and we shared cookouts and birthday parties. But, as I say, something transpired in the midst of the Cedar Fire that made us intimates in a different way, witnesses of life-changing circumstances. On Tuesday evening, October 28, 2003, high up in the Cuyamaca Mountains of San Diego, deep within the fiery furnace of the Cedar Fire, there was a colossal manifestation of God's presence. It transformed all of our lives.

I can only call it a miracle. The dictionary defines a miracle as: **1.** An event that appears inexplicable by the laws of nature, held to be supernatural in origin or an act of God. **2.** One that excites admiring awe. Philosophers and theologians have debated whether miracles take place for thousands of years. I am not going to provide another installment in that debate here. Instead, I've attempted to report what I experienced. Skeptics are free to doubt, but as you will see, something took place, and that something was so odd, so strange, that it defies reasonable natural explanation. It is a story I have told to many people, and over the years I've often been confronted by tearful faces. Such reactions planted a seed in me to write this book.

It may be that you have never given God a second thought. Or, perhaps you can be found front and center every Sunday morning in your local church. Either way, my assignment is the same. It is simply to tell you my story, to describe truthfully and accurately the things I have touched with my hands, seen with my eyes, and heard with my ears.

The story begins with a prayer. Not a mild powerless wish, but a bold headlong leap.

A leap of faith.

The people, places and events within this book are real. Many of the names have been changed and a few minor characters are composites, but story is true.

Come with me behind the curtain.

Lord, I have heard the news about you; I am amazed at what you have done. Lord, do great things once again in our time; make those things happen again in our own days.

(Habakkuk 3:2) MSG

GOD
INSIDE THE FIRE

An Amazing True Story

GREG STELLEY

I

THE CEDAR FIRE

Chapter One
Manna Season

The most beautiful thing we can experience in life is the mysterious. It is the source of all true art and science. He to whom this emotion is a stranger, who can no longer pause to wonder and stand rapt in awe, is as good as dead: for his eyes are closed.

ALBERT EINSTEIN

Chapter One
Manna Season

WAIKIKI, HAWAII, SEPTEMBER 2003
2:15 A.M.
A FULL MOON beamed down onto the shimmering water below Diamond Head. And through the window of a 12th story beach front hotel room, yellow stripes of moonlight bent around the form of a woman and her husband asleep in bed. The woman was dreaming...

A tall blond woman in the middle of a mountain road. Flames are everywhere. She's holding her hands high. Something's coming! She's screaming! Wait...wait...That's Kathy! Frank's behind her. He's running to help! He's too late!

Joni bolted up in bed—breathless. "There's going to be a fire, Greg."

"*Huh?*" I whispered.

"I had a dream. I saw Kathy and Frank. They were in the middle of it."

"Joni, honey, there's 2,500 miles of ocean between us and San Diego right now. Call Kathy when the sun comes up, okay? Besides, they didn't die in your dream, right?"

"No."

"What about Veronica? The rest of the kids?"

"No, I didn't see any of them." She smiled, beginning to feel better.

"Good." I grinned. "Then they've got a chance!" She laughed. "Joni, If you ever dream *I'm* about to die, let it be a surprise, okay?" She gave me a tearful look of her lovely green eyes. "Ahhh, you'd look at me like that and I'd know I was a dead man."

She checked on our daughters, Danielle, 9, and Juliette, 8, as they slept in the other bed.

I closed my eyes and tried to get back to sleep. By now, I was quite accustomed to Joni's episodes of precognition. She had suffered a seemingly fatal head injury when she was hit and pinned under a moving car at the age of two. The doctors had done what they could, but she wasn't expected to *live*, much less walk or talk. She'd always told me that it was God, *himself* who had miraculously healed her after the accident. That may have had something to do with it. All I knew was that she saw things before they happened. And that wasn't all. Joni could read people. The woman could see right through a person—could see their *sins*, even. The Bible calls it spiritual discernment. I just called it life with Joni.

I, myself had sometimes witnessed glimpses of what I knew to be the impossible—brief flashes of a type of power and love that I knew for certain was not of this world. But what was coming wasn't a glimpse and it wasn't a flash. It was a flurry of impossibilities that rained down upon my family like manna from heaven for an entire *season*—the fall of 2003. It began one month before the Cedar Fire, during a blissful Hawaiian day at the beach.

BELLOWS BEACH

Danielle, brunette, tall for her age, and Juliette, blond, cute and bubbly, sat talking together in the rear seat of our rental jeep as I drove along the leeward side of Oahu. Both of them were wearing identical new pairs of beautiful polarized sunglasses.

Joni, sporting her *own* stylish pair, sat in the passenger seat. She turned to me as I drove, the tropical sun glinting off *my* new polarized Maui Jims.

"You still mad?" she asked.

"A sunglass salesman. On the beach."

"He came up and handed them to me. *Really!* I just wanted to try them," Joni explained.

"And $800 later... *Joni.* All right, I'll give it a rest. Just don't wear them into the surf, okay? We don't have neck bands for them yet."

The sand on Bellows Beach sparkled like sugar. I waded into the aquamarine ocean water, ducked under a roller and popped up. Joni, on her wave board, was angling straight toward me on a three-foot breaker. She pushed down on the left side of the board and changed directions. That's when I saw the sun sparkle off her expensive new sunglasses. A few minutes later came the inevitable.

"Can you tell me where you were when you lost them?" I asked through gritted teeth while standing in three feet of salt water.

Joni looked at me with sad resignation. She turned and sloshed her way out of the ocean.

I began shuffling my feet back and forth in the loose grainy sand below the surf, feeling my way along, hoping to chance upon those two-hundred dollar Maui Jims. For an hour I shuffled, big rollers lifting me up and pushing me down the beach, but it was hopeless — like trying to find an expensive needle in a shifting, surging, underwater haystack.

I trudged out of the water past Danielle and Juliette playing in the shore break. When I reached my wife she was standing in the shade of a cypress tree. I stood there, dripping, warm sand clinging to my feet, and itching for an argument. Joni wouldn't take the bait. Instead, she marched briskly back toward the water without saying a word. And she began to pray.

Lord, Greg was right and you know how he is about money. He's never going to forgive me. I need your help! Please, Lord, will you help me find my glasses? Now?

I watched Joni slosh into knee high ocean water. She paused for a moment, then turned her body directly toward me — 50 feet away on the beach. Joni stared straight ahead. I had no idea what was was about to happen, but I sensed something. I couldn't take my eyes off of her. She sidestepped two feet to her left, paused a few seconds, then without looking down, dropped to a squat, jamming her hands through the water and deep into the loose sugary coral sand. Down they went, diving eight inches or so into the seabed. She took a hold of something with both hands, jerked that something up out of the sand and the water and placed her *g l a s s e s* directly onto her face!

I stood in stunned amazement.

My hand covered my mouth. I splashed my way over to her, shaking my head. "Oh my God! Oh my *God!* That was a*maz*ing! *Amazing!*

My wife looked me in the eye. "I knew you wouldn't forgive me so I asked God to help me find them."

I told her I was wrong to have been so upset with her and she gave me a hug. Later that afternoon, we bought four bands and attached them to the glasses.

The rest of our days on Oahu were spent on the beach, on the water, or snorkeling under it.

Danielle, making like a mermaid at Hanauma Bay, came up briefly for air in front of me. "C'mon, Dad, follow me!"

I watched her flip forward, her legs sliding into the warm clear water three feet below the surface. I followed after her. We swam through undersea valleys and grottos, passing the homes of multicolored tropical fish who kept a wary eye on us as we snorkeled by. Danielle waited for me, then grabbed my arm and pointed to a beautiful iridescent fish. It changed color with each movement in the sunlit water. She called it the rainbow fish.

On the flight home, Joni sat across from me in a middle row. The girls sat between us. We had checked four pieces of luggage and stowed three pieces of carry on, but the most valuable item we brought home with us was one that could never have been on the plane without the Lord's help. Joni's faith in Him to accomplish the impossible—the hopeless, was dangling by the band around her neck.

"I talked to Kathy this morning," said Joni. "She wants us to come up Saturday and see their new place in the mountains."

"Fine by me," I replied.

It was the first day of October 2003, and San Diego was less than a month away from catastrophe. In truth, what happened on Bellows Beach would prove to be little more than an appetizer to God's seven course dinner. He had long planned the miraculous meal that was about to be served to the Stelley and Scalari families. The Lord had begun preparations two years earlier with an unlikely trio of ingredients: A cowboy, a horse, and an 11-year-old girl...

LAKESIDE, CA.

MAY 2001

Time seemed to slow for Kyle Ripp—always did at this point. His chaps rippled in the dusty breeze with each pounding hoof beat of his favorite stallion. He grasped thick leather reins in a gloved right hand and stood up in the stirrups twirling a nylon rope over his head just like his daddy had taught him at the age of seven. His father had loved and respected horses. Kyle, on the other hand, enjoyed seeing fear in an animal's eyes. Pain was his shortcut to obedience.

"Shut off your ears, son. Focus." So Kyle focused. And just as he had done for the past three decades, he shut off his ears.

The little brown mustang in front of him was fast. More than fast, the horse was terrified. The mustang knew what came next and was frantic to escape it. The animal slowed in the turn and Kyle caught him around the right foreleg with a lightening quick stab of his rope. The little brown horse tumbled head first, doing an awkward barrel roll in the process.

Ripp pulled a pack of Winston's from his right breast pocket and tapped it against his glove as he stood over the helpless horse on the ground. He lit a match. Kyle took a long draw from his fresh smoke, then flicked the flaming match onto the mustang's side.

"Cheap target practice. That's all you're good for, you wild piece a' shit."

He untied the homely little gelding. The mustang scrabbled back onto his hooves and bolted to the far side of the arena.

23

Late in the afternoon Kyle's roping shoulder began bothering him. He'd had enough. The limping, bleeding, mustang obediently followed the man into the barn and a filthy stall. Kyle clanked the stall gate shut.

Around six in the evening Kyle pulled a wagon loaded with alfalfa down the center of the barn's breezeway. He threw flakes to horses on either side, then paused in front of the mustang's stall. Ripp looked into the tormented animal's eyes, then rolled the wagon past the hungry horse straining at the gate.

A few days later, John Parker, 35, in a tan uniform with chrome and gold badge affixed, bumped along a dusty dirt road in a green government pickup, pulling a horse trailer. The sticker on the driver door read: U.S. DEPT. OF INTERIOR BUREAU OF LAND MANAGEMENT. The agent pulled up near Kyle's arena and got out. The rodeo circuit rider was waiting.

"John, back so soon?"

"Where's my mustang, Kyle?"

"That's *my* mustang, John. You know that. I paid a hundred and thirty-five dollars for him at your auction. I got a receipt!"

"He's government property for a year after you adopt him. Has it been a year, Kyle? Bring him to me."

Kyle brought the limping mustang out to John, dried blood caked around his hooves. The horse was thin and weak. John glared at Kyle in disgust. He took the lead rope from him and walked the battered horse toward the trailer.

"I want my money back! Where's my money!" Kyle bellowed.

John squinted. "You'll be lucky if I don't put you in jail."

PARKER RANCH, JAMUL, CA.

Kathy Scalari, 39, a tall, blond, mother of four, stood grasping the top of a four-rail pipe corral with her 11-year-old daughter, Veronica. John Parker and Kathy Scalari traveled in the same local horse circle so news of the pitiful mustang didn't take long to reach her animal loving daughter. John ambled up to the two of them.

"Morning, John. How have you been?" asked Kathy. "We heard about this poor mustang you took back and Veronica wanted to come see him."

John's bay mare was at that moment pressing herself into the corner of the pipe corral nearest Veronica. Whatever silent code the horse was sending, the lanky golden-haired girl was effortlessly deciphering.

"Her rear hoof is bothering her. She needs it picked—could be a rock," said Veronica.

"I'll take a look at it. Thanks," said John. "Looks like you have a budding horse trainer with you today, Kathy. So, Veronica, do you really want to see the mustang?"

John had grown accustomed to seeing the results of cruelty to his mustangs over the years, but this horse's physical and mental condition was so poor that it set a new low for inhumane treatment. He walked the two of them over to the traumatized horse pacing frantically inside an isolated corral.

"Once we started feeding him he was strong enough to fight back. He's safe now, but he doesn't know it," said John.

Veronica inched her way toward the corral. The lathered mustang paced in a circle, his eyes flashing wildly. The girl opened her palms, lifted her hands high and began to coo like a dove. John became fascinated as he watched her work her magic. The mustang perked his ears toward the gentle sound of her voice. Suddenly, the horse jolted sideways as if being shocked.

"*Easy!* That's close enough!" said John as he lunged forward, pulling the girl back to a safe distance.

"What's going to happen to him?" asked Kathy.

"He's not adoptable. Jumped out of the corral yesterday at the *sight* of a rope. I'm gonna' have to put him down."

"*Mom!* We can't just let him die!" pleaded Veronica.

"But 'Ron. Look at him! He's crazy. Not even *you* can fix a crazy horse."

"Mom! *Please!* I connected with him. He's not crazy. He doesn't trust people, that's all. I can help him. I *know* I can. Please?"

Kathy searched her daughter's dark brown eyes and found herself at eleven again, pleading with *her* mother. She decided to reverse the curse. "John, it's up to you. What do you say?"

John was dubious. This mustang was dangerous. A single .38 round to the head was the safest solution. His mind was made up. His mouth, however, didn't follow the script.

"You can try, Veronica, I'll let you try," said John, "I'll bring him over to you tomorrow morning."

NEO

Grandma Tammy, 60, stood next to Kathy in the shade of her long covered porch. The mother and daughter were witness to an odd sight. Veronica was standing with her back to the wild mustang's corral, forty feet or so behind her. She peeked over her shoulder at the mustang. Slowly, patiently, she took one step backwards and stopped. She waited. She took another step.

Tammy shook her head. "That's the damnedest thing. My granddaughter steppin' backwards for a horse. A *mustang* no less!" Tammy had seen enough. She turned away.

Kathy winced as the front screen door slammed shut with a bounce. Old battle lines drawn with Tammy decades before remained unresolved today. Mother and daughter had never even tried talking peace. Kathy had given up wondering why. Instead, she simply stopped returning fire. That was the best she could do.

Step after backwards step Kathy watched her daughter's tedious progress toward the isolated corral and the horse inside of it.

The mustang remained calm. There was no threat from the *back*side of a human. The man had never hurt him while walking away. Twenty excruciating minutes later, Veronica finally reached the horse.

"Here I am pretty boy. Don't be afraid. Look, I brought you something good."

Veronica opened her hand and offered some oat mix to the mustang. He hesitated, tickling the girl's hand with his whiskers. She reached over with her other hand and stroked his muzzle. He began to eat. "See, you just needed a new start, huh." *New? No...Neo.*

"Neo. How's that? I'm going to call you Neo."

The horse bobbed and neighed. Kathy tiptoed up to her daughter and her new friend. "Neo, huh? I like it."

The damaged horse with the short black mane soon began to trust the skinny girl with the golden locks. At first, Veronica would simply spend time near him, talking to him, touching him. By mid-October, 2002, Neo would allow Veronica to lead him with a halter and lead rope. By April, the mustang could be saddled and would take the bit. During that time, Kathy, her husband Frank, and their other three children spent countless hours at Tammy's ranch attending to the Scalari's other horses. All the while, Neo's confidence in Veronica slowly continued to climb.

<hr />

MAY 2003

Frank Scalari, a 43-year-old physicist, sat in his office chunking away on a computer keyboard with ear buds in place and heavy metal music cranking. He had escaped his Sicilian roots in upstate New York in the 1980s when, against his mother's wishes, he had accepted an invitation to a West Coast grad school. One Friday night, his frat brothers talked him into closing his science books to come with them to a dance club. He met a girl there. Kathy was tall, blonde and beautiful. A West Coast Madonna. It was over for Frank. She was the one. Four kids later, Frank was already weary of the harness. His Uncle Leo had warned him about this...

A family man is like a plow horse, Frankie. He keeps his head down. He never looks up. He doesn't want to know how much ground there's left to plow.

To his right, next to the computer screen, sat a burl-framed photo Christmas card. It had been taken last December at Grandma Tammy's. Neo was at center of it in a snow covered corral. The horse sported a Santa hat cocked at a jaunty angle while six smiling Scalari elves with pointy ears and red felt hats surrounded him. The names in gold letters read: *Frank, Kathy, Frankie, Veronica, Alex,* and the smallest elf, *Anna.* It had snowed that morning, a rare occurrence in San Diego's high foothills, so the whole family had raced the sun to decorate with lights and tinsel. Frank remembered setting the timer on his camera then racing to Neo, who startled, which caused his Santa hat to slip.

It was hilarious. It was perfect.

Frank was a well paid, heavy hitting computer scientist on a daily quest for useful algorithms. He was exceedingly patient — like a cleanup hitter who walked to the plate, calmly waited for his pitch, then smacked it out of the park.

Sean Cain, 24, the beautiful, meticulously groomed owner-founder of Technomitry Software, the *latest* company to acquire Frank's contract, passed by a row of cubicles with his Greater Swiss Mountain dog at his side. The occupants popped up like dandelions behind him. Cain strolled into Frank's office...

"Didn't you get my e-mail? I need you to lean forward on this project, Frank. I promised you'd demo our new inventory prototype in January. The technology convention?"

Both men watched the mammoth dog lift his leg over Frank's potted cornstalk plant.

Frank glared at Sean. He shook his head. "It'll be close — I won't be able to fireproof it."

"It's got to be perfect. Maybe I should've brought in someone younger," smirked Sean.

"No! You knew who you were getting when you brought me here. It's my prototype. It'll be perfect."

"It better be, old man." said Sean. He yanked the dog back and disappeared out the door.

Frank stared down at the framed Christmas photo. Neo stared back at him. It had been two full years since his oldest daughter had rescued the hopeless horse and Frank still didn't understand why. So much time and effort. Still, he had to admire her. *That's one lucky mustang,* thought Frank.

He turned up the music, put his shoulder into it, and resumed plowing.

Veronica sat on the saddled mustang within the riding ring. Joni and I stood alongside our friends, Kathy and Frank, our hands grasping the top rail. Danielle, Juliette, and the rest of the Scalari's kids, Frankie, Alex, and Anna stood scattered around the oval-shaped arena. We had been following Veronica's patient work with Neo for two years. Today was going to put that work to the test.

"Give him a kick," Kathy said to her daughter.

"Show us what he's got, Veronica," urged Frank.

Veronica clicked her tongue and kicked Neo with both heels. Everyone began to clap. The mustang began to trot, then to lope. Veronica stood up in the stirrups, flaxen hair flying, as the swift little horse looped around the ring. We all sent up a loud cheer.

"Atta boy Neo!" said Veronica as she patted his neck.

"Good job, honey!" Frank said, beaming with pride.

I gave him a knuckle bump. All of us were proud of Veronica. We were impressed with what her love had brought about, but her triumph only brought another problem into sharper focus. Frank and Kathy had been renting a house not far from Tammy's ranch while they conducted a four year search for an ideal horse property. Over the course of those four years they had looked at one piece of land after another, never quite finding the right one. Meanwhile, prices had skyrocketed. Now they were forced to expand their quest to the north and to the east.

"Any luck finding that perfect horse ranch?" I asked. "You know you're my favorite scientist, Doc, but you make too much money to be renting."

Frank laughed. "They don't teach economics to grad school physics students, Greg. Some of us academics are really just savants you know—heads in the clouds and feet off the ground. But, no luck yet. We're still looking."

Joni clanked the gate shut behind Veronica and Neo. "He looks like a smooth ride."

Veronica loosened his bridle. "He's got a little hitch in his trot but a really soft lope. I was surprised."

Kathy unlatched the saddle's belly strap. "I think I found us a place, Joni. I just haven't found the right way to tell Frank about it."

Joni smiled. "I've been praying you'd find one."

A jackass brayed in the background... *Haw-he-haw-he-haw*

Kathy laughed uncomfortably. "Thanks?"

Joni teased Kathy with hands to her face: "The 'P' word? *Not the 'P' word! Aaaah!*"

It had gone on like that for years. These two seemingly mismatched friends forgave one another their spiritual foolishness. Kathy pardoned Joni for believing in Father, Son, and Holy Spirit, and Joni overlooked Kathy's belief in whatever new "secret" or "code" was being currently displayed in book store windows. Joni was open with Kathy about her love for the Lord, and Kathy was just as open about not accepting the Bible as supernaturally inspired. Both believed the other stood on spiritual quicksand. Joni never gave up, and Kathy never gave in.

"Joni, you don't really believe in the devil do you? Do you actually believe hell is a real place? Ha! Nobody burns forever in a literal hell when they die!"

"Yes, Kathy. Hell exists. Jesus taught about it, and I trust him."

On that warm afternoon in early June 2003, only God himself could've foreseen the horrors that loomed ahead of us in late October. As it turned out, Kathy had just found the piece of property that would change all of our lives forever.

MANNA SEASON

Chapter Two
Cuyamaca

Cuyamaca is evidently a Spanish corruption of the Indian words Ah-ha' Kwe-ah-mac (Water Beyond), a name used by the Indians, first to designate a location high on the middle mountain, but afterward applied to the entire group.

These mountains had distinctive names also. The one farthest north they called E-yee (Nest), because they believed that a big nest or den was on one of its slopes in which the wild animals disappeared when hunted, thus safely evading pursuit. The middle one, Hal-kwo-kwilsh' (Tough Strong), gained this title in the battle of the peaks, when he proved very formidable. The one known as Cuyamaca Peak, acquired the name Poo-kwoo-sqwee' (Crooked Neck) in the same battle.

MARY ELIZABETH JOHNSON 1914

Poo-Kwoo
Sqwee'

Crooked
Neck

CUYAMACA PEAK

Chapter Two
Cuyamaca

KATHY HEARD FRANK'S old pickup shudder to a stop.

"There's your Dad, Frankie. Go help him with the groceries."

Frank came through the kitchen door, grasping plastic bags in each hand as Frankie struggled in behind him.

Kathy waited as Frank put down the last bag. "I found another property. It's five acres or so, but there's one thing. It's off the grid."

"Where is it this time?" Frank asked.

"Cuyamaca Woods, not too far from Julian."

He frowned, "It's a long drive to anywhere from there, Kath."

"Let's just go look at it."

"We must have driven by it before. Is it on Engineers Road?"

"Uh-huh."

It clicked. Frank knew exactly where it was. "That's 'way up there, I'm thinking, 4,000 feet! I'll have to buy Frankie a snow shovel for Christmas!"

"Cool! Snow!" said Frankie. The other three kids streamed into the kitchen, little five-year-old Anna latching onto her Daddy's leg. They all wanted to see the house.

"OK,"surrendered Frank. "The commute would be a drag, but we'll look."

Kathy arranged a weekend appointment with the listing agent.

SAN DIEGO/ THE CUYAMACAS

LAKE CUYAMACA

After breakfast, Frank and his family piled into their Suburban and began the one-hour trip from Jamul to Cuyamaca. The half-hour uphill drive eastward on Interstate 8 brought them to the off ramp Frank was looking for, and he turned left under the Interstate onto Highway 79, the winding two-lane road through Cuyamaca State Park. Soon, tall pines dominated the landscape mixed with green meadows, running streams and massive oaks. The surrounding peaks revealed large granite boulders. Just ahead, Lake Cuyamaca shimmered in the midmorning sun.

They passed a chalet-style restaurant at the western end of the lake. "Look, the Edelweiss is still in business," Kathy said. A mile north, Alex, the nine-year-old, lowered his window as they drove past the boat dock. The whine of outboard motors echoed off the surrounding mountains. A small bait store sat twenty feet above the dock just off the highway. A mile farther north they ran out of lake.

"There's the fire station. And that's Engineers Road," said Kathy.

Frank drove past the small volunteer fire station on the right. Within a minute's drive uphill, the family drove into a dense, dark, pine forest. Frank flipped on the headlights. The homes within the forest were largely hidden from view. Frank drove the last three miles of switch backs as they slowly descended from above 5,000 feet to just under 4,000. Kathy spotted the open green gate the man from the real estate office had mentioned.

The real estate agent was waiting for them in his car parked near the barn. The agent, in his late fifties, was tall and lanky in blue jeans and snakeskin boots. He walked over to them.

"Hello folks. You're Kathy, right? And *you*, sir, must be *Mr.* Scalari."

"Frank."

"Fine crop of youngsters you've got there, Frank."

Alex spotted a long swing hanging from a huge oak tree directly in front of the house. Kathy asked the agent if was okay, then the children began taking turns standing on the wood plank seat, swinging out on a long low arc while grasping nylon ropes that hung from a massive limb twenty feet above.

"You folks like apples?" the agent asked. "Because you'll have an orchard of them." He took Frank and Kathy to the orchard just north of the barn. "I hope you know how to bake an apple pie," he joked. The agent twisted an apple off a branch and handed one to Kathy. "Mmm! These are good! Here Frank, take a bite!"

Frank glared down at the agent's rattlesnake boots, then at the rose-and-green colored piece of fruit in Kathy's right hand. She stood there, arm extended, smiling. He glanced over at the agent, grinning at him from ear to ear. Frank took a chomp of her apple. It *was* good.

"How far does the property continue beyond the apple orchard?" Frank asked.

The agent pointed due north: "You see that access road about two hundred yards north of here? Well, that's the easement for the other property owners around you. Your property is inside of that road as it circles around the house."

Frank nodded, "So the access road is the property line."

"Pretty close, Mr. Scalari. You might want to hire a surveyor just to make sure. Lemme show you your power plant before we see the house."

Frank and the agent ducked inside the low door of the pump house. They inspected row after row of batteries fed by the photo voltaic panels outside. These, along with a diesel generator, were the only sources of power for the house. The air inside the pump house smelled sweet. The batteries were clicking with electricity. Frank remembered this pleasant aroma from his childhood, standing on a kitchen chair when he was four, watching his mother mix a batch of cookies in her old Sunbeam mixer—its blue current arcing inside the motor. He smelled the same scent then that he smelled now. Ozone.

It was time to inspect the house. Built 150 feet behind the barn on a slight rise, a five-foot high cinder block foundation at the front transitioned to ground level in the rear. The Scalari children watched impatiently as three adults trudged up the stairs to the open-air balcony with the extended eave overhang. The agent punched in the lock-box code, unlocked the door and got out of the way. The four children scrambled in across the family room and dashed up the polished wood staircase to look at the bedrooms.

"Kath, come see this," said Frank.

She met him at the south end of the downstairs.

He pointed. "Look, a big fireplace and a potbellied stove." The black iron stove was across the room near the base of the stairs.

They climbed the staircase and inspected the master bedroom and the third story loft, then were shown out the back. Kathy spotted a problem. "Look at all those trees. They're dead."

Frank stepped off the landing and walked toward the tall dead pines just inside the eastern property line near the dirt driveway. Some stood beside a chain link fence along the southern property line just 20 feet or so away from the house.

"There's a bunch of them," Frank said as he began to count. "I count 13. Are those inside the property line?"

"Yes, I'm afraid those dead pines are going to be Job One before you'll get fire insurance." The agent paused to reset his grin.

"So is that chain link fence over there on the property line?" Frank asked.

The agent sighed, "Maybe yes and maybe no. There are quite a few inaccurate fences around this mountain. You'll need a survey done to know for sure."

The Scalaris climbed into the Suburban for the ride home.

"We're going to talk it over," Frank told the agent. "We'll let you know if we're going to make an offer."

"Let me know soon. I don't think this one will be on the market very long."

Frank waited for the green gate to open and aimed the Suburban uphill for the long ride home. Kathy polled the kids as they headed out. It was unanimous in favor of the move, with Veronica rating it a "strong buy."

Kathy turned toward her husband. "That loft would make a nice office for you, don't you think?"

Frank thought it over. No doubt about it. The house was perfect. The property was gorgeous. A house powered by the sun—*just* perfect for a green-minded scientist like Frank. It was, in fact, everything he and Kathy had been longing for. Best of all, his children had become euphoric the moment they'd arrived. There would be plenty of room for their kids and their horses and who knew how many other animals Veronica might end up collecting with so much space. Frank could give them all the childhood he'd missed out on. And he could say yes to Kathy. After years of searching, he could finally say yes to her paradise – the Shangri-La she had discovered. There were only two catches though they seemed minor. The dead pines would have to be dealt with, and they would need to get an accurate survey to be certain of the property lines. Surely not a problem. A slight smile appeared at the corner of Frank's mouth.

"What do you think we should offer?" he said finally.

Kathy yipped for joy. The Suburban rocked as the children whooped and hollered. Within the week their offer was accepted. The Scalari's new home in the mountains was in escrow.

MOUNTAIN HOME   SEPTEMBER 2003

Escrow closed on the 1st of September for the Scalaris, and after a week of moving, they quickly discovered the joys of living in their mountain home to be as wonderful as they'd anticipated. In the mornings, the mountain comes alive with the sounds of birds at the top of the pines greeting the first rays of sunlight in a joyful symphony of praise. The evenings are cool and invigorating. Frank and Kathy were certain they'd taken possession of some kind of fairy tale existence. True enough. The Cuyamaca's are full of fairy tales – all of them involving long-ago Indians.

Frankie sat at the breakfast table slurping a bowl of cereal while staring at his laptop. On the screen was a book cover: **INDIAN LEGENDS OF THE CUYAMACA MOUNTAINS by Mary Elizabeth Johnson**. It had been copyrighted in 1914. He scrolled down to the foreword page and read aloud as he traced with an index finger.

"Cuyamaca – a Spanish corruption of the Indian words: 'Ah-ha Kwe-ah-mac.' It means 'Water Beyond,' or 'The Place Where It Rains.' The northern mountain, that's *our* mountain, was called E-yee' – 'Nest' in English. It says Indian hunting parties watched deer and wild turkey disappear over here."

"Interesting," said Kathy. "Did the Indians live up here year 'round?"

Frankie continued to read. "They lived in a big village called Helsh-ow' Na-wa.' In English, 'Rabbit House.' It stood at the base of Cuyamaca Peak. When the winter snows came they'd ride their horses down to another village on the beach. They'd go fishing for a few months."

Veronica burst through the front balcony door. "The tree cutters are here!"

The crew began their work. The smallest of them climbed 80 feet up the first pine tree with pulley and rope. He pulled up a chain saw, started it, then cut the top four feet off the dead tree. He whistled a warning to the other men as it fell to the ground with a resounding thump. Kathy and Frank knew that the temporary fire insurance policy the seller had purchased during escrow would expire in a few weeks. All thirteen dead pines had to be cut down and they had to pass the insurance agent's inspection before a new policy could be issued. Frank had hired this crew to do it.

Veronica rushed into the kitchen to the muffled sound of chain saws. "Frankie saddled Neo and Cindy. We're ready to ride, but Frankie's got Indians in his brain."

Kathy handed her two folded paper bags. "I packed a couple of snacks for you. Tell your brother to watch for mountain lions, not Indians. *Stay on the trail.*"

Veronica rode Neo and Frankie rode Cindy, Kathy's palomino, down Engineers Road. They quickly came face to face with a man and a woman on horseback, sauntering forward from the opposite direction. The four riders stopped — the horses nose to nose.

"You're our new neighbors," said the man, in his fifties.

"Yeah, we just moved in. I'm Frankie and this is Veronica."

"I'm Tom. This is Sharon, my wife. And right there, that's our place." Tom pointed to a two-story log house with a barn nearby.

"Where you kids headed this morning?" asked Sharon.

"We heard about a trail beside a creek," said Veronica.

"Tom and I were on that trail this morning. You'll love it! Just follow this road until you reach Boulder Creek Road, turn right, then look for the trailhead marker."

Frankie and Veronica followed Boulder Creek Road until they spotted a weathered marker for a trailhead.

"I hear water. Let's try this one," said Frankie, pulling reins to the right. He led them down a descending forest trail full of towering pines, incense cedars and wild blackberries. Shadows broken by moving dapples of sunlight appeared, then disappeared, and at the bottom they found a flowing brook. Colorful rocks filled the stream bed. This was Ah-ha-'Mi-Ah-ha,' or in English, Water Colder Water, the one mentioned in his Indian book. Frankie splashed his mare to the middle of the brook, then Veronica and Neo came alongside. The sound of rushing, gurgling water filled their ears.

"Frankie?"

"Shhhh," Frankie whispered, thinking he had heard something else. Faintly, very faintly, Frankie thought he could make out a kind of music playing softly through the babble of the water. Indian flute music. He stared ahead, enchanted, transported to another time. The 16-year-old boy closed his eyes...

Indian maidens appeared up and down the stream, many of them bathing—giggling in the cold water. Others washed deerskin clothing on rocks at the water's edge. Full baskets of acorns sat nearby. A lovely dark-eyed Indian girl stood up from her bath. She gave Frankie a smile...

Veronica wondered why her brother was grinning from ear to ear. Frankie opened his eyes—the Indian girls were gone—replaced by the babble of the water and the sound of the pines in the steady breeze. In the middle of the stream, 100 feet in front of them, a mother mule deer and her fawn stood at the base of a small waterfall. The doe took a long cold drink. Her white speckled fawn began to nurse. Veronica thought it was the most beautiful thing she had ever seen. Neo bobbed and gave a low whinny. The deer startled, sprang out of the brook and disappeared into dark forest. Neo craned his head around and looked into the eyes of the golden-haired girl on his back. For Veronica, it was a special moment. Two years ago she had granted Neo pardon just as his execution was at hand. The mustang hadn't deserved it, she had simply granted it. Today, Neo had given *himself* to the girl. He had done so willingly.

"Let's head home, Neo," said Veronica.

Mountain
Pines

"Softly
Intoning
Their
Prayers
to the
Heavens
Above"

Ah-ha′ Wi-Ah-ha′ (Water Colder Water)

The Cold Spring, located on the high peak of the Cuyamacas, is well known to all lovers of these mountains, and the Indians, who must ever have a reason for the existence of things, tell how it was created and named by one of their mythical creatures of long ago.

AT one time in the ages past, the Ah-ha′ Kwe-ah-mac′ (Water Beyond) mountains were infested by monstrous giants with loathsome, ill-shapen bodies, who terrorized the surrounding country. These marauders, lurking and watching their opportunity, frequently stole the Indian maids from their villages, keeping them in bondage as slaves.

One of the giants, named Hum-am′ Kwish′wash (Whip to Kill People), lived in the vicinity of Pam-mum′am-wah′ (Green Valley).

He reveled in the most fiendish ogrisms, but his innate sense of the beautiful was keen and strong. He not only selected the most delightful places in which to live, but surrounded himself with objects pleasing to the eye. Always he stole the fairest of the Indian maids, and required them to weave the most exquisite designs known in their art of basket making.

41

We had just returned from Hawaii the day we first saw the Scalari's new place in the mountains. It was a bright Saturday morning and the Cuyamacas were a feast for the eyes. As we crested North Peak in our diesel pickup, I glanced at Joni in the passenger seat. She was wearing the sunglasses she had miraculously retrieved from the bottom of the ocean one week earlier.

Much of the time, our lives appear to be guided by random chance—the people we meet, the friends we make. And from all appearances it had been random chance, nothing more, that first brought Joni and I together with Frank and Kathy Scalari in 1989. We were just two young married couples who happened to buy new houses at the same time on the same street. Over the years, an unusual friendship developed. The four of us did not agree on issues of faith, or in the existence of the supernatural, but we clicked for some reason. None of us could've put a finger on it that early October day in 2003, but as I look back on it now, several years after the Cedar Fire, it was a divine destiny that brought the Stelleys and Scalaris together.

Joni peered out the windshield. "We're looking for a green gate, Greg."

"Yes, Miss Joni, a gate that is green. Danielle? Juliette? A little help for your Dad?

"There it is!" Juliette had spotted it.

When we first entered the green gate I took a look at the massive oak tree in front of the house. Alex was flying out full-tilt on the swing that hung from the huge oak's lower branch. Danielle and Juliette hopped out of the truck and ran toward a short line of Scalari children waiting for a turn on the swing.

"Hi guys! Bye guys!" Alex called to us as he flew out to the end of the swing's arc, halfway to the barn. Below him, Veronica's black hen, Chocolate, scratched for bugs. For an instant, Alex was suspended at a 35-degree angle. *Chocolate!* he screamed as he was pulled back into the shadows of the old oak's canopy.

The southern neighboring acreage near the barn was overgrown with tall yellow weeds and dead brush. We drove around the entire property on a dirt road, passing by the orchard as three horses lazily munched on apples. After slowly rolling past the big pasture I veered to the right, then followed the rutted dirt road around past multiple power panels facing south in the sunlight. A jumbled stack of cut branches, maybe 100 feet long, were piled close to the road. I turned toward the rear of the house, passing between the pile of branches on the right and an enormous pile of *logs* on the left of the dirt driveway. Frank and Kathy and stepped off the back porch to welcome us.

"Hey, you made it!" said Kathy.

"What a great spot you two found," I said. "I do have *one* question for you. What do you do when you just need bread and milk? It's 30 miles to town!"

Frank chuckled. "We drive to the bait store up at the lake. That's Cuyamaca's 'supermarket.' C'mon, I'll show you around."

Frank showed me his power shed with its rows of what looked like car batteries, clicking with electricity, being filled to capacity by the photovoltaic cells outside. Frank was happy to explain how it all worked. Frankie came up as the two of us examined the goat pen. Two young males were rearing up, crashing skulls together.

"Stupid goats." Frankie muttered.

"Don't let your sister hear you say that," said Frank.

"Why goats, Frank?" I asked. "I mean, I get the horses and the chickens, but goats?"

"They belong to Veronica and Alex," Frank said. "We get milk and cheese from the females. Soap too. Veronica breeds and sells them. It's a good little business for a kid."

The three of us walked south near the long pile of branches and kindling. I stopped along the way and lifted a pine branch from the top of the stack. Its dry brown needles fell to the ground.

"You get your fire insurance?"

"The agent is coming next week," said Frank. "We followed his requirements to the letter. We'll pass, I'm sure."

I shook my head looking at all that dry wood. "What's the difference between the dead trees standing, or the wood *cut* from all those trees stacked on the ground? It seems to me it's a worse fire hazard now."

Frank stroked his chin. "I wonder about that myself. All I know is we did what they asked us to do."

We drifted over to the back side of the house and the rear porch, then crossed the dirt driveway to the massive stack of tree trunks piled two feet over our heads.

"It looks like you're opening a firewood business, Frank. You've got that old truck. You could fill the bed with wood and park by a main road."

"I'll need someone to *split* all these logs, Greg." He looked at me and began to laugh. "I'll pay you in firewood."

"Sounds like a deal." I looked around the property. "Frank, you really have found the promised land here."

He smiled. "One problem. See that chain link fence behind the wood? It's five feet inside our neighbor's property — right where all the logs are stacked. Surveyor found it. We're going to have to replace the fence — preferably after we burn all this firewood."

Meanwhile, Kathy and Joni were in the orchard, surrounded by the sweet fragrance of ripe apples.

"I know we're a long drive for you," Kathy apologized.

"Oh Kathy, it's a beautiful spot. I think you did the right thing. God puts us right where he wants us."

"Ummm..."

Joni stood quietly, holding her ground. She lifted an apple-filled branch to her nose. She sniffed. Suddenly, the sky went dark...

The branch was on fire. Her hand too. Strange flames chased up and down her arm. She looked to the barn and saw huge flames pouring out of the open breezeway. It exploded into glittering metal pieces before her eyes...

She let go of the branch. The flames disappeared. Joni grabbed the left side of her head, wincing in pain.

"What happened? You okay? *Joni!*"

Joni didn't respond. After a moment the blinding pain subsided.

"I'm all right. I get headaches sometimes, that's all. Sometimes I... I... see things."

"You see things?"

"Yes, since I was a kid. I told you about my car accident, didn't I? When I was two? My dad was a Marine, so we lived on base at Camp Pendleton when I was little. That day, the street was filled with kids on tricycles while moms and off duty dads supervised. My mother left me with a baby-sitter for the first time that morning to do some shopping. As she returned, she stepped off the bus with her groceries at the end of our street. A drunk woman in a car made a screeching turn, almost hitting her. Mom spotted me as I stepped up to the sidewalk and she screamed for me to run, but it was too late. The car jumped the curb and ran over me. The woman kept driving. I was still pinned underneath."

Kathy's mouth dropped. "Oh my *God!* Joni!"

"Five Marines lifted the car off of me, then another Marine, one of my dad's friends, took off his shirt and pressed it against my skull until they got me to the hospital."

"I'm amazed you even survived."

"The *doctors* couldn't figure out why I was still alive. The neurosurgeon wasn't optimistic even after he finished my surgery. He told my parents: 'Your daughter has suffered a major head injury. She lost a large amount of brain fluid. She may never walk, or even talk again. She may live a week, she may live a year, but I've done all I can do. The rest is up to God.' That's what he told them, Kathy. I've been living on borrowed time since I was two-years-old. *God's* time."

"But Joni, you don't actually believe..."

"In the power of God? I don't have any choice. Not since that day. Sometimes He gives me warnings, pictures of things to come. I never ask for them, God just sends them."

"What did you see?" Kathy asked. "You looked horrified."

"Ummm... Just a flash of something. Bright colors. I can't say any more."

"Why not? What did you see?"

"I don't know yet. I have to wait."

Veronica, Alex, Anna, Danielle and Juliette were inside the breezeway of the barn busily brushing and grooming Neo. He neighed his approval. Chocolate, Veronica's black hen waddled in, bobbing and clucking on the ground between Neo's front hooves.

"Chocolate! Hello baby!" said Veronica.

Neo gently nuzzled the chicken. Chocolate cocked an orange eye up at Neo, then flew up with a squawk, landing between the mustang's ears. Neo jerked his head up, taking Chocolate for a fast ride. She clucked—flapping her wings as she went, and Alex doubled over with laughter, holding his sides.

Frank and I joined Kathy and Joni in the middle of the apple orchard. I scanned the scene—the barn, the house, and the horse pasture beyond us.

I looked to Joni. *See, everything's okay. It was just a dream this time. It doesn't have to come true.*

Kathy plucked a ripe, rose-and-green apple. "These are Julian apples. Try one."

I crunched into it. "Sweet and tangy. Very good!"

"C'mon. Let's show you the house," said Frank.

So the four of us stood in the midst of the orchard munching apples in the midday sun, watching our children swing out halfway to the barn. The Scalari's new place seemed a treasured field upon a chosen mountain. It seemed *that* day that it might always remain so.

CUYAMACA

CINDY, SKIP & NEO LOOK FOR APPLES   VERONICA
NEO THE WILD MUSTANG   & NEO

Chapter Three
The Cedar Fire

You are probably quite right in thinking that you will never see a miracle done: They come on great occasions: they are found at the great ganglions of history—not of political or social history, but of that spiritual history which cannot be fully known by men.

C.S. LEWIS

Chapter Three
The Cedar Fire

SATURDAY, OCTOBER 25TH, 2003
SUNRISE

THE SUN ROSE sharply from the eastern horizon. The air crackled with static electricity. The Santa Ana wind, a very strong, dry wind from the East, was howling at 50 miles an hour. Far out in the Pacific Ocean, halfway to Hawaii, a low-pressure front with warm temperatures had stalled. Now, a super bullet train of cold air rushed southwest from 700 miles away at Utah's Great Salt Lake. The fierce wind raced up and over the 10,000-foot-high San Bernardino Mountains. The rapid speed of the wind as it channeled up and over mountains 10,000 feet high, caused enormous friction, heating up the air like a space shuttle on reentry.

A true Santa Ana condition such as this one is rare. The surest confirmation is air temperature. The beaches were 100°F degrees that day. Mountain temperatures were in the 90s. San Diego's coastal air conditioner, the onshore breeze, had been switched off. Surfers straddled their boards, bobbing beyond the surf line, just beating the heat. No one was surfing that morning. The waves were being decapitated, blown back at the top of the curl. To the uninitiated, it was a crystal blue, hot, dry, windy morning, but to the native-born, it was a time to pray.

8:50 A.M.

I stepped outside our house and scanned the sky warily. No smoke yet. Mornings like this one bring a particular form of dread. It's like working in a fireworks factory when the lights go out. *You* know better than to strike a match, your friends know better, but it just takes one dimwitted fool. The devil wind was howling, the fuel was in place, just waiting for a spark—a ricocheting bullet, a backfire, an arsonist, or that dimwitted fool. I climbed into my truck and headed down to the pool store in El Cajon. I needed chlorine.

OCEAN BEACH

On the beach near the Ocean Beach Pier, a young, very pale couple struggled to spread beach towels in the scorching wind. Bill and Jenny Bright were strangers to San Diego—two newlyweds who were a long way from home. Jenny, 24, was a blond, blue-eyed, surgical nurse from London, and Bill, 26, was 'a lucky man indeed,' as his mates used to tell him.

Jenny sat up on her towel in a sheer leopard print bikini. It was more revealing than she was comfortable wearing, but Billy had bought it for her and he liked seeing her in it. A tune by Coldplay blared from the radio at the foot of Jenny's beach towel. The DJ stepped on the intro:

"It's hot out there folks. The beaches are already over a hundred. Santa Ana conditions are going to be with us for a few days so be extra careful in the back country. Please, no open flames of any kind."

Bill gawked at the surf. The tops of breakers were being sheared off—blown backwards. "Strange weather, this, Jenny. Nothin' ever like it back home," he said as he rubbed sunscreen on her shoulder blades.

Jenny dropped her bikini straps and held her top in place with her hand. "Marry a nurse and see the world, huh, Billy-luv. It's a two-year contract, like it or not."

Billy rubbed.

Jenny peered down at the white stripes on her red shoulders. "*Look!* Our last free Saturday and I'm burning to a crisp!"

9:10 A.M.

I came through the glass doors of the pool supply store and brought the Santa Ana winds in with me. I drifted past the inflatable rafts and the pool toys to the back of the store where the chlorine was stocked. An older man and his wife were standing in the aisle. The man, in his seventies, turned to me, a bottle of chlorine in each hand.

"Gonna' be a bad one I'm afraid. You a native?"

"Yes, sir, we're a dying breed."

He smiled. "I haven't seen devil winds this strong since the Laguna Fire. September 1970."

"Yeah, I remember that fire. I was thirteen. We couldn't breathe — the *smoke.*"

The man's wife, a beautiful woman in her sixties, became alarmed. "Maybe we should cancel our flight, Roy. I mean...if you think we *should*," she said, her eyes pleading no.

Roy gave her a lustful look. "After forty years with an old bronc buster like me? No Bev, you and me are flying to Maui tomorrow morning, just like we planned."

"You two have a great trip."

Roy leaned in and needled me with an elbow. "Youuu *betcha!* She's had our bags packed for a week!" He gave me a wry smile and a wink.

10:00 A.M.

Up the mountain in Cuyamaca Woods, Kathy stepped outside onto the balcony and into a strong northeasterly gale. Gusts above 50 miles an hour were bending the pines over to the southwest at a 30-degree angle. Unsecured objects were flying across the yard. Kathy looked up at the sharp, clear, blue sky. *Nothing yet. Please let it stay that way,* she thought. She watched a white wooden bar stool go airborne a little north of the barn. It slammed part way through the old hog wire fence on the western property line. It hung where the fence caught it, quivering in the wind—appearing to levitate a foot off the ground.

Kathy answered the phone.

"Kathy? It's Joni. Are you all right? Do you see any smoke?"

Kathy scanned the sky. "No, no smoke yet. We're okay for now, but the wind is really blowing up here. Maybe we'll get lucky again, huh?"

"No. No luck. Time's up," said Joni.

"What do you mean, time's up? Don't *say* things like that!"

"Time...is...*up*. You need to listen to me, Kathy. I've been having dreams about fire. A really *terrible* fire. I didn't want to frighten you that day in the apple orchard. I wanted to be wrong about it. But now... *Oh Kathy!* I wish it wasn't true!"

Kathy began to tremble. "*What!* You wish *what* wasn't true? You're freaking me out!"

"You're in great danger! It's your house, Kathy! I saw the orchard on fire! I saw your barn burning to the ground! Your mountain's going to *burn!*"

2:15 P.M.

Beverly Piper, 68, sat in a lounge chair next to her pool wearing a navy blue one piece swimsuit. She was reading a book. Her broad hat flapped in the wind, straining against the chin strap. Her husband Roy, 72, stood tanned and leathery in swim trunks as he walked the length of their pool, a plastic jug in his left hand, glugging chlorine into the water as he went. To his right, ten feet below the black pool fence, sat Wildcat Canyon Road.

Bill and Jenny Bright were headed home after a fairly miserable day at the beach. The wind was too hot, the water was too cold, and both of them were quite sunburned. The employment agency back home in London had found a rental house for them online before they ever boarded the plane for San Diego. It was located a little east of Roy and Bev's on Wildcat Canyon Road. Bill slowed around the last turn for home. Jenny spotted Roy above the road as he walked along his pool fence.

"There's that sweet old codger with the bitchy old wife," sniped Jenny, waving to Roy.

Bill tapped a friendly honk as they drove by. Roy smiled and waved vigorously. Bev peered up from her reading glasses to shoot darts at him.

"It's that English couple, Bev. What are their names again?"

"Bill and Jenny. She's a nurse, remember? You seem to be quite impressed with her."

"I waved, Bev. That's all. C'mon, don't be mad."

CEDAR CREEK   4:30 P.M.

Deer season officially opened that morning, but almost every hunter recognized the dangerous conditions and stayed home. *Almost* every hunter. Two deer hunting friends from Orange County had been trudging around since early morning in the high brush just to the north of Cedar Creek. The creek splits Cuyamaca Woods from its northern neighbor, Pine Hills, one mountain over. The wilderness between the two mountains had not burned in 50 years. Dry thick undergrowth crowded in around the oak trees and the manzanita. The two hunters had planned this trip for over a month, and although conditions could scarcely be worse, neither of them called it off.

A wrong turn late in the afternoon had left the friends separated. An empty canteen clunked against the lost hunter's belly, the result of shortsighted guzzling earlier in the day. He broke through a ten-foot-high thicket of chaparral. Dirty and dehydrated and panicky, he'd found a rocky flat—a clearing in the maze. He scrambled to the top of a large, smooth granite boulder and took a breather. He tried his cell phone again. No service. He stood up and called out for his friend, but his voice was lost in the hot gusting gale. He brought his right hand to his brow to block the glare as he focused as far down his line of sight as he could. The clear dry air allowed him to see sharply all the way to the western horizon out at sea. He spotted a small brown crescent of land *far* out in the Pacific Ocean, Santa Catalina Island. He wished he were there, or anywhere else where there were people, roads, cold drinks, hot food, and familiar faces happy to see him.

The sun was low in the southwestern sky. A pack of coyotes

55

crept up on a big jackrabbit from hidden trails just below the clearing. The rabbit's piercing screams and the pack's excited yelps filled the hunter's terrified ears. He began to sob, his head buried in crossed arms. Afraid to leave his clearing, and too dehydrated to hike anywhere, and what was more, not knowing where to hike, he wanted more than anything to go home to his wife, his kids, and his comfortable bed.

After an hour, true panic set in and he simply could not imagine being left alone all night. He was desperate and willing to do anything. He gathered dead wood, twigs and dry grass from the surrounding area, piled them high in the middle of the clearing, and did the unthinkable.

He lit a fire.

Within minutes, the flames had grown to 20 feet high, blowing sideways on the wind. The escaping fire set the surrounding brush aflame. The man watched in horror, but it was too late. What he had done could not be undone.

A sheriff's rescue helicopter was in the air at that moment searching for a lost man in the area. The lost hunter's partner had hiked back to his truck and called 911 on his cell phone. Ten minutes after the first flame kindled, the sheriff's helicopter crested a high ridge. What a deputy-pilot named Dave, and his copilot, Rocky, saw below them soured their stomachs.

"Rocky! There's a fire down there!" Dave blurted into his headset mic.

"Dammit! And there's our lost hunter. He's waving his arms," said Rocky, focusing his binoculars upwind of the flames.

Dave glanced at the setting sun. Maybe there was still time. "Ramona base, This is Sheriff Rescue requesting tanker support. We have a small brush fire... I repeat, a small brush fire in the Cedar Creek area near Pine Hills. Over."

"Roger that," said the California Department of Forestry dispatcher.

Rocky wasn't optimistic. "They're not gonna' send 'em Dave, it's too close to dark."

The two pilots sat looking at each other. They were hovering over what they knew would become a catastrophe. The radio was silent. The fire below continued to grow before the pilot's eyes. It was heartbreaking.

"Sheriff Rescue. This is Ramona base. Negative for the tanker. CDF flight rules, boys. It's too close to dark. I've got some pilots down here that are mad as hornets! Sorry. Ramona base out."

Nothing could be done now except to rescue the man near the fire.

"Do you see him?" Rocky asked.

"I've got him. Let go upwind of him and see if we can set down."

They spotted a clearing nearby. Sheriff Dave set the copter down on it, surrounded by 10-foot-high chaparral. The two pilots got out and began hacking their way to the lost man, 50 yards away. The flames were moving steadily to the west now. Minutes later, the two sheriff's pilots broke through a wall of prickly brush. There he was. They found him lying down, unable to stand. Sheriff Rocky opened a plastic water bottle and watched as he took a long drink.

"I thought I was gonna die!" he confessed, after guzzling down a second bottle of water.

"Did you start the fire? Asked the pilot.

"I'm sorry about all of this," said the man, who tried to stand, but fell down.

The pilots helped him up and reentered the painful brush with the hunter supported between them. When they got back to the helicopter, the sunlight was all but gone. The sheriffs hoisted the man into a rear jump seat, strapped him in and took off. The copter rose into the smoke filled sky. What the pilots saw below them filled their hearts with anguish. In the time it took them to retrieve this man, the fire had grown from an acre to nearly twenty. Suddenly, a strong gust of wind blew the chopper sideways to the southwest.

"Sheriff Rescue to dispatch."

"Go ahead Sheriff Rescue."

"Dispatch, I'm requesting immediate evacuations southeast of Ramona. We don't have much time, Carla... Over."

"10-4 Sheriff Rescue. We'll call everyone out ASAP."

Sheriff Dave wheeled the copter around and headed for Ramona. During the ride back, Rocky, the copilot, again spoke to the culpable man in the jump seat.

"Do you know what you've done? Nothing will be able to stop that fire now. *Nothing!* Why did you do it?"

The man wouldn't look up at either of them. He didn't say another word to them. Back on the ground, he gave his personal information to law enforcement officers, but without enough evidence to charge him, he and his friend were released. Neither man said much during the hour and a half trip back to Orange County. Soon, he was home again, reunited with his family.

9:00 P.M.

By nine, the fire was still burning in uninhabited areas, but the wind had picked up again. That there was a fire raging was scarcely known because the fire started so close to dusk that its enormous, 10,000 foot high smoke plume, which would have alerted the entire county during the day, was unseen and unknown in the dark. The on-duty firemen for the California Department of Forestry knew about the fire but the genie was out of the bottle. The wind conditions were so horrific and the location of the wildfire was so inaccessible that the first engine companies dispatched from Ramona couldn't get anywhere near the flames. Their only focus was to warn as many people as they could down wind of the fire. Lives were at stake and the firemen knew it. Police were beginning evacuations.

11:00 P.M.

Saturday evening at the Stelley place, our family sat listening to flying debris from outside slam into the stucco walls of our home. The strong wind sounded like a desolate train's whistle as strong gusts resonated through every gap in the eaves. Joni and I sat watching a local television channel around eleven when these words moved across the bottom of the screen:

THIS IS A WILDFIRE WARNING FOR RESIDENTS IN RAMONA COUNTRY ESTATES AND RAMONA. BE ADVISED. A WILDFIRE IS BURNING NORTHEAST OF THESE AREAS. BE PREPARED TO EVACUATE AT ONCE.

Joni grabbed the phone. "Hello, Kathy? Are you okay?"

"We're okay," said Kathy. "The wind is blowing the fire away from us. We don't even have any smoke."

While they were talking, a local news reporter broke in with the first sketchy news of the wildfire: "It is being reported that parts of the community of Ramona Country Estates are burning," the reporter stated. "This fire is being called the Cedar Fire because it began near Cedar Creek in a place called Pine Hills, east of Ramona. We don't yet know how this fire started." Kathy saw the same newscast. "Joni, this is going to be a terrible fire."

"Kathy, people are going to die in this fire tonight."

WILDCAT CANYON   3:07 A.M.

The Cedar Fire exploded like a bomb. What was a 5,500 acre, back country wildfire at midnight, had transformed into a 62,000 acre mushroom-cloud of a firestorm. The wildfire had become eleven times larger in just three hours. The monstrous inferno was barreling forward on the stiff wind directly over the northern end of the town of Lakeside.

All along Wildcat Canyon Road it was raining horizontal fire. Bill and Jenny Bright were asleep—unaware their house was in the middle of a fiery blizzard. Jenny was having a nightmare. She was dressed in surgical scrubs in an operating room, surrounded by a team of surgeons—Americans all, and every one of them was smoking. She was suffocating. *The operating theater is so hot!* Jenny choked. Her head pounded. She began to gag. She opened her eyes. The smoke alarm was blaring. The room was bright orange. *Something's wrong!* Smoke poured from the walls around the bed. Blue flames licked around the door jamb.

"BILLY! FIRE!"

Bill lurched out of bed wearing only pajama bottoms. Jenny jumped to her feet in a short teddy and panties.

"Don't open the door!" screamed Bill. He grabbed the car keys off the night stand, raced to the window, opened it and popped out the screen. "Jen! C'mon! *Now!*"

Jenny was desperately rummaging through a chest-of-drawers. "Let me put some clothes on!" The loud crackle of fire filled her ears from the other side of the bedroom door.

Bill grabbed Jenny around the waist and pulled her to the window. He picked her up and threw her outside into a raging inferno. He leapt out after her. Then the bedroom exploded.

The two of them ran barefoot through a gauntlet of flames around the fully engulfed house, desperate to reach the safety inside their car. It was all that mattered. Not the excruciating heat, not the shower of red hot embers pelting against bare skin, but only the hope of escape. Jenny tripped over a sprinkler and sprawled onto a low hedge. Bill grabbed her hand, pulled her to her feet and kept going. He began frantically pushing the unlock button on his car keys. Jenny stood bouncing impatiently outside the passenger door.

"BILLY! HURRY!"

A constant shower of glowing cinders caught in her blonde hair. She focused on the door lock. It popped up. The newlyweds slid into their seats and Bill started the engine.

A few houses to the west, Roy and Beverly Piper were sound asleep. They had gone to bed before nine to awake very early for their 6:30 a.m. flight to Hawaii. The digital alarm clock on Bev's night stand read 3:19. It flipped to 3:20. A man's voice jolted Bev awake:

"The firestorm is burning rapidly through the Barona Indian Reservation and is headed for northern Lakeside. If you know anyone in that area..."

Bev punched the radio off. "Roy! Are you awake?"

"Yeah, I heard it."

Roy and Beverly shuffled stiffly into their 1970s era living room wearing slippers and bedclothes. A look of wide-eyed terror formed on Bev's orangy face as she gazed out the bay window.

"Oh no! Oh my God! *No!*"

Gigantic wind-whipped flames were visible down at the west end of the canyon. A constant torrent of embers flowed left to right headed southwest across the big window. The Cedar Fire was passing over them. Roy was calm and direct: "Get your purse. Nothing else. There's no time."

"Just let me grab my pictures!" Bev insisted.

"There's no *time*, Bev. We've got to go!" Roy grabbed his wallet and keys off the top of the entrance table, then pushed Beverly toward the kitchen stairs to the garage. He took a long glance at their suitcases sitting near the top step—he had tucked their airline tickets through one of the handles last night. Roy turned away and hurried Bev down the stairs to the car. The garage door slowly rolled up and revealed flames burning on the hillsides above their home. A small blue car passed by on the road below, headed west. It was Bill and Jenny. Roy slammed the car in reverse, spun around on the concrete apron and headed down his driveway for Wildcat Canyon Road.

Bill and Jenny gaped out the windshield at an unimaginable sight. Huge fire twisters, low in the canyon, were spinning their way uphill toward the road, half a mile in front of them. Bill drove toward them anyway, not knowing what else to do. The fierce wind moved the swirling towers of flame to the left, then to the right across the asphalt, two hundred feet ahead.

Tears streamed down Jenny's beautiful face. *Why did we come here? It's all my fault.* She wished she was back home in London, locked outside in an ice storm. Anyplace but here. She focused on her bare toes—on her painted toenails. Jenny's feet touched the hot floorboard. They jerked backwards.

Bill slammed on the brakes. He stared wide-eyed out the windshield. *There's no way out!* A wall of flames blocked both lanes of the road. Smoke began spewing from the A/C vents. Jenny became hysterical.

"Billy! *Billy!* We're dead! We're *dead!*"

Roy was driving like he always did around a notorious blind curve on Wildcat Canyon Road—*too fast.* Bev let him know about it like *she* always did—loudly.

"Roy! Slow down! I see brake lights!"

Roy locked up the brakes, skidding to a stop.

A small blue sedan was stopped dead in the middle of the road in front of them. A one-hundred-foot-high vortex of flame swirled before it. Two frantically moving silhouettes inside of it were backlit by the advancing wall of revolving fire.

"That's Bill and Jenny! I recognize their car!" cried Roy.

"They're just sitting there!" Bev anguished, remembering the faces of the young newlyweds. "Maybe they need our help!"

Roy grabbed for the metal door handle. His burn reflex threw his hand back at him like a live frog in a boiling pot. "We can't! It's too hot out there!"

Jenny, the registered nurse, searched for a life-preserving solution to their grim prognosis. When none could be found, she simply lost it. She began clawing Billy with her fingernails.

"I'm not ready! Billy! Don't let me die! I don't want to die!"

Bill was quite calm about it.

"We can't stay here, Jen.' We've got to go."

"WHERE!" shrieked Jenny.

"There." said Billy, cocking his head toward the wall of rotating flames. "I've got to drive us through it. NOW!" Bill punched the gas pedal, lurching both of them back in their seats.

Jenny screamed.

Roy and Bev watched the brake lights from their neighbor's car go out. The car rapidly accelerated, then disappeared behind the hot curtain of fire.

"They're going to die in there!" shrieked Bev.

"Maybe they'll make it," said Roy, not liking their chances.

Bill was driving blind. Orange tongues of fire glided smoothly over the windshield. Hot streamers of yellow flame rollicked along the side windows. The shrill screech of Jenny's screams filled the hot air inside the car. The road curved sharply to the left, but Billy drove straight ahead. The car left the asphalt, careening along a rocky apron. Jenny lurched and bounced along as the flaming car hurdled toward a steep drop off. Bill yanked the wheel at the last second. They crashed into a blazing tree.

Sheets of sweat poured off of Jenny and Bill. He tried to restart the engine, but the wiring had burned through. It was over.

Jenny stopped screaming. Her eyes flashed. Her mind flew with frenzied thoughts — good memories, nothing but good ones. Then her beautiful blue eyes stopped. They softened. She surrendered to her fate. "Come here, Billy-luv."

He slid over to her, buried his head between her breasts and wept uncontrollably. She pulled him tight to her chest. He began shaking violently as she stroked his hair.

"I'm so sorry, Jen, I'm so sorry."

She spoke haltingly, tearfully. "I...only...re-mem-ber...one pra-yer. Mum prayed it with me when I was a little girl... *Now I lay me down to sleep, I pray the Lord my soul to keep! Amen!*"

CRASH! Every car window exploded. Flames filled the car. Bill and Jenny swayed in the midst of the flames—still embracing.

Roy sat idling as Bill and Jenny had done, staring into the deadly fire curtain spread across Wildcat Canyon Road. The flames parted briefly and he caught a glimpse of Bill and Jenny's disabled car 100 yards inside of it, black smoke pouring out of blown-out windows.

Die right now, or keep trying to live. It was an easy choice when he thought about it. Roy turned toward Beverly. He leveled with her.

"We've got to go back, darlin.' I've got an idea, but you've gotta trust me." He backed up, turned the car around and put it in drive.

Roy punched the gas pedal, but then slammed on the brakes. He rested his head against the steering wheel and closed his eyes. He didn't know what to do. Which way led to life?

Maybe it won't work. Maybe I should try to drive us out of here.

Beverly became frantic during his moment of indecision. She gazed out the rear window. Arching, yellow, jagged flames filled the glass. Her ears filled with terrible sounds penetrating through the car windows—a thunderous rolling and crackling, then a peculiar hissing.

WHOOSH!

A purple-yellow explosion from deep inside the flames, 100 yards down the fiery road, rocked their idling car on its springs. Bill and Jenny's fuel tank had exploded. The 20-foot-wide spherical eruption rolled skyward. Caught by the wind, it traveled westward like a burning, runaway hot air balloon.

"I trust you! *Punch it!*" screamed Bev.

Roy drove uphill to the east, dodging careening cars coming west, lurching wildly with tires blazing. Bev gaped at the wide-eyed drivers. Their mouths were wide open. They were screaming for their lives.

Flames stalked from behind them as Roy drove up his driveway.

He dashed into his garage and sprinted to his workbench.

"Yes, here you are! I knew you were here!" he said aloud to a piece of coiled copper tubing left over from the central A/C installation years ago. His hands shook as he urgently uncurled it to it's full six foot length, then he carefully cut it in half with a pipe cutter.

Outside again, the old man handed one of the three-foot tubes to his bride. "We're going into the pool! C'mon!" he yelled over the crackling wind.

Roy and Beverly leaned into the blizzard. A steady blast of red embers blew past, burning their faces as they hurried around their home to the backyard. The black aluminum latch was hot to Roy's fingers as he opened the pool gate. Tongues of sixty-foot flames from the canyon below licked at their Tipuana trees, twenty feet away. Bev squeezed her copper tube with both hands and watched her husband search their false stream bed for two of the biggest river rocks he could carry. Roy hurriedly heaved one, then the other into the pool's deep end.

"Oh, I hope you don't hurt your back," Bev said softly. Tears streamed down her face when she caught the desperate irony of her concern.

Roy came to her side and cupped his bleeding, shaking hands to her ear. "I'll tell you when to jump. When I say, you dive down to the bottom, find a rock, squeeze your ankles around it, then point your tube out of the water and blow as hard as you can. That'll clear the water out."

The two held hands and prayed. Roy asked God to protect them as the fire passed over them. He had to yell over the rolling crackle of the flames.

"I love you, little filly."

"My sweet cowboy."

They both laughed through their tears. He held her in his arms and kissed her. The heat became unbearable long before the flames reached them.

"*Now! Jump now!*" screamed Roy.

He watched his wife take a deep breath and dive to the bottom. A few seconds later, he saw her tube pop above the water. A moment passed, then water came gushing out of it.

"Good girl! It works!" he said to himself.

Roy quickly splashed thick lounge cushions onto the surface of the pool's deep end. The heat from huge flames 50 feet away began to blister his skin.

"Now, or never," he said calmly with a shrug.

He drew in as much smoky air as he could, then down he dove into the water, clutching his tube. At the bottom, he felt blindly for his rock. Twenty-seconds of searching. Nothing. His old lungs ached for relief. Finally, he bumped into his wife's leg with his forehead. She pulled him up with her free hand and wrapped his arm around her waist. He squeezed her rock with his ankles and pushed his remaining breath into his tube with a hearty chug.

4:07 A.M.

Joni could not sleep. She'd watched a local TV news channel's sketchy reports on the fire through the wee hours of Sunday morning. A young female anchor tossed to a reporter who stood on a high ridge above a canyon floor. Huge flames flared behind him.

"This fire shows no signs of slowing down. Wildcat Canyon, below me, is burning. We can only hope that all the people somehow managed to get out before it was too late," said the reporter.

As he spoke, embers shot up over the ridge behind him. Joni saw fear in the man's eyes.

"Jamie, we've got to leave! Flames are coming uphill behind me!"

4:15 A.M.

Two feet above Bev and Roy's underwater hiding place the thatched bamboo roof of the bar at the shallow end was blazing like a giant tiki torch, along with the lounge chairs, the fiberglass diving board, even the plastic pipes and the pump. The lounge cushions above the couple's heads acted like air filters as they pressed their breathing tubes against the wet undersides of them. The air was very hot and smoky, and it scorched their throats if they took anything but the shallowest breaths, but they were still alive. Minutes passed like hours while they waited below. No words were possible and none were needed. Above them, the agony was over for any living thing remaining in the fiery furnace that was Wildcat Canyon. The fervent heat two feet above them was not survivable.

"What should I be thinking about as I'm in the process of cheating death?" Roy wondered. He was sure that he should be thinking profound thoughts. Flashbacks of the essence of his time on earth. His wedding night with the beautiful, frisky, 25-year-old Bev. The birth of their two sons. Instead, he kept thinking about each breath, each gifted second of consciousness. Each painful, labored, inhalation of the poisonous air was a victory. The more it hurt, the more his head pounded, the more thankful to God he became for the time. He wanted more of it.

Bev was not much aware of her physical pain. It hurt to breathe, all right, but she ignored it. She pushed it far into the background of her mind. Instead, she began to free herself from the burden she'd been carrying and then delivering to others for most of her 68 years. With each breath she drew, she was letting go. She was forgiving someone, erasing their offenses from the slate board of her soul. When she was finished forgiving, she began burning the slate board, along with the markers hung on a wire above it—her tabulated history to be called upon when needed to justify her negative opinion of someone. Lastly, she forgave Roy for never earning her respect. Then she asked God to forgive her for never giving it. He had earned it tonight. This was his shining moment. He was saving her life. She clung to him, the two of them standing intertwined in an underwater embrace as intimate an act of love and protection as they had ever experienced, but the act of breathing in the wretched, scalding air was becoming intolerable.

Breathe! Roy commanded his lungs.

The pool water was brightly lit from the flames, heating dramatically and quickly darkening with sooted embers and black smoke. Roy closed his eyes under the hot water close to the surface and was surprised by what his mind's eye was displaying to him. The strange sight of this odd crustacean made logical sense to him after a second or two. He was picturing a live, boiling lobster. He began to sympathize with all the lobsters dunked into scalding water at his request during the last 50 years.

Seventy minutes after they entered the water the glow from the fire above the surface diminished. They popped their heads above the water. Roy shoved the burned shells of the lounge cushions toward the shallow end.

"Where is our house? Where did it go?" Bev cried, her voice cracking.

Their two-story home was now a one story high pile of flaming debris. "We're alive! We're *alive!* That's all that matters!" Roy shouted.

They waded through filthy water toward the shallow end, and when they reached the steps Roy began splashing water over the hot concrete lip to cool it. He took off his shirt and wiped the area clean of soot.

"Sit here darlin,'" he told Bev. Then he sat down beside her. Small flames still crackled behind them in the strong wind. Bev stared at Roy for a long time, at his beautiful rugged face, softened by the fire's orange glow.

"We should be dead," she said softly, tears running down her face.

He looked into her eyes. After all these years her beauty still amazed him. "We're still here, little filly. It didn't get us."

He stared down into the canyon at hundreds of bright red hot spots scattered throughout the chasm. Farther west, a wall of enormous flames played leapfrog in the darkness on strong gusts of fast moving air. He was as tired as he could ever remember, but an overwhelming peace settled upon him. He was content. With his life. *Just* his life.

As the first morning light began to reveal the devastation, he wrapped both arms around his wet, shivering wife. She buried her face in his chest.

"Let's just sit here and watch the sunrise," he said to her.

She didn't say anything for a long time.

Scripps Ranch
Sunday morning, October 26, 2003

JOHN GIBBINS/Union-Tribune

JOHN GASTALDO/Union-Tribune

Southern California burning, 10/26/2003

El Cajon, Ca. Sunday night, 10/26/2003   SALLY WALKER PHOTO

Chapter Four
City In Flames

Surely wickedness burns like a fire; it consumes briers and thorns, it sets the forest thickets ablaze, so that it rolls upward in a column of smoke.

(Isaiah 9:18)

Chapter Four
City In Flames

SUNDAY, OCTOBER 26, 2003

6:30 A.M.

THE FIRESTORM ENTERED the northeastern boundary of the City of San Diego a few minutes after sunrise. San Diego Fire Rescue dispatched fifty engine companies and eleven brush rigs in response to the fire, but the wind conditions were so ghastly that the firemen could do little more than hurriedly evacuate residents in the immediate path of the firestorm.

By mid Sunday morning, the entire country was watching Fox News and CNN as the Cedar Fire exploded into Scripps Ranch, a community of multimillion dollar homes 30 minutes northeast of downtown San Diego. Wind whipped towers of flame raced up and out of brushy canyons to the east and made quick work of entire cul-de-sac's, reducing homes to blackened chimneys with manicured lawns. The wood shake shingles on most of the homes doomed them to destruction.

The fire continued traveling southwest, straight and true with the dry Santa Ana wind. Desperately needed tanker aircraft were being used on another large wildfire in Los Angeles County. By midday, the fire had jumped west of Interstate 15 at Miramar Naval Air Station in the middle of the county. Flames raced forward into the open space which buffers the base from the surrounding homes.

The sun had become a burnt orange smudge in the smoke filled sky. Light conditions were so dim that motorists flipped on their headlights. A million residents downwind of the fire were forced to breathe this poisoned soup in shallow gulps as pounds of embers and ash blew into every yard. Satellite images showed the Cedar Fire's smoke plume extending hundreds of miles out to sea. Meanwhile, a desperate run on air purifiers emptied every store shelf of them within the day.

Northern California, Texas, Arizona, Oregon and other western states graciously dispatched firefighters and equipment to help, although most wouldn't arrive until Monday. The wind hadn't let up and thousands of homes were now directly in the southwest path of the inferno. Late Sunday afternoon the firestorm jumped to the west of Interstate 805. Now, only Interstate 5 stood between the fire and the ocean. It appeared that the Cedar Fire would not stop until it reached the surf.

But by four that afternoon, the wind stopped as quickly as it started. It just quit. A dead calm descended over San Diego, the ashtray of the world. A perfect tipping point in the brown sky above had been reached. The flames died down, squatting in place. Then, slowly, burning embers began falling to the *east* of the flames.

Children, quarantined inside all day, ventured out into city streets with palms open, catching ash like snowflakes.

During the night of the 26th, the fire and the land called a shaky truce. The flames ran in place, the humidity rose, but by the next morning the truce had ended.

MONDAY, OCTOBER 27, 2003

SUNRISE

The onshore breeze suddenly returned. The firestorm doubled back toward the east, burning south of the previous day's destructive swath. Fire companies from other states arrived and were soon dispatched to defendable neighborhoods in the onrushing fire's path. The fire fighters set up perimeters, rescued people, foamed houses, bulldozed firebreaks, and made hard decisions about which houses they would fight to save and which houses would be left to burn. Wise homeowners quickly cleared a 100-foot ring around their homes. Homes with shake shingles, overhanging trees and close high brush weren't likely to survive.

The burning edge of The Cedar Fire was now 30 miles long and no containment was possible. By the end of the day, flames had burned homes in Tierra Santa, northeast of Qualcomm Stadium, Santee, and Lakeside, all of them to the north of the widest, most defendable, north-south firebreak in the county, Interstate 8. Kathy and Frank, 3,500 feet higher on a western slope of the Cuyamacas, were preparing for the worst.

7:45 A.M.

Kathy glanced nervously at her watch. "C'mon Alex! Get your shoes on and get in the car! It's almost eight! We've got to go!"

Veronica was in a panic. She came up breathlessly to her dad as he and Frankie loaded the last of the goats into the trailer.

"*Dad!* I can't find Chocolate!"

"I thought we had all the chickens," Frank said.

"Frankie, have you seen her?" asked Veronica.

"No, not since yesterday morning. Anna threw out some scratch. She was with the other chickens."

Chocolate, the small black hen, had a history of disappearing from time to time. Fox, the dog, had killed another chicken this morning. Now, Chocolate was missing.

"Anna, have you seen Chocolate?" asked Veronica.

Her little sister was talking happily to several chickens inside crates

75

on the ground. "Cinnamon? Did you see Choc'lette today?" said the 5-year-old, imagining the speckled hen's response.

Buk, buk, buk.

The western sky was filled with towering smoke. It was chugging forward like a slow, inevitable freight train. No brakes. No way to stop it.

Kathy stood over one of the crates filled with chickens. "C'mon, Veronica, help me! It's time to go!"

"We *can't* go, Mom, we have to find her!" she said as she helped Kathy hoist the last crate full of chickens into the hay bin at the front of the trailer.

"Honey, we *have* to go. You know how Chocolate is. She could be anywhere. Dad and I are coming back later for the horses. I promise we'll look for her, okay?"

Veronica walked back into the barn. "Chocolate? Here chick, chick. *Please* come out."

Frank honked the horn. Neo bobbed and neighed from his stall. Veronica stroked his muzzle. Her eyes widened. Frank honked again — *twice* this time. She bolted out of the barn and ran to the Suburban.

"Mom! Dad! We can't leave!"

Frank didn't want to hear it. "Veronica! Inside the car! *Now!*"

"But *Dad!* You don't understand!"

Kathy had heard enough. "Do what your father told you to do!"

Veronica clammed up. She took a seat next to Anna in the middle row and folded her arms across her waist. They rolled past the barn, then through the green gate, and Veronica began to cry.

The trip to Grandma Tammy's home in Jamul was foreboding. Cuyamaca still looked beautiful today. Mule deer grazed in a meadow. Pine trees sang *shhhhhhhh* in the steady breeze, and Golden Eagles flew lazy eights high in the blue sky. Anna stared out her window as they passed the bait store at the lake, the deserted dock below full of bobbing boats.

"Will our house be okay, Momma?" Anna asked. Her unblinking brown eyes waited for an answer.

"I don't know, honey. I hope so." Kathy smiled, though her eyes brimmed with tears. A dark vision of her home and property in flames flashed silently in her mind.

Veronica gazed out her window at Lake Cuyamaca's shimmering blue surface. A garland of tall green pines surrounded it. Tears traced down her cheeks. Frank glanced at her in the rearview mirror.

"Ron? I hate to see you cry. This is hard on all of us. Please tell Daddy what's wrong."

"It's too late, Dad. It's Neo. We should've taken him this trip."

"Your dad and I are coming back for the horses later," said Kathy.

Veronica shook her head. "You'll never get him into the trailer. Even I have trouble. He's not going to make it."

A half-hour later and 2,000 feet lower, Frank drove down Interstate 8 and into the teeth of the firestorm.

"The traffic isn't moving up ahead," said Frank. He came to an abrupt stop.

The Highway Patrol had created a traffic break just two minutes earlier in the westbound lanes. Several fire engine companies were positioned on the freeway in an attempt to contain the fire to the north of the Interstate. Jagged, roaring, orange and yellow flames licked at the edge of I-8 as it burned uphill from below. Several aircraft were en route to this new southern edge of the Cedar Fire, including two air tankers and one helicopter reassigned from an uncontrollable fire burning in the uninhabited foothills below the Cuyamacas. If the firemen failed, if the flames crossed to the southern side of the freeway, there was nothing but open country all the way to Grandma Tammy's ranch in Jamul.

Kathy opened her front passenger door and stood up on the running board. "I can see the firemen," she said to her children. "There's a lot of them."

She saw more than 100 men in yellow and brown fire suits spraying thousands of gallons of water at the rising flames. She grabbed some field glasses from under her front seat and focused sharply on the life-and-death drama happening 10 car-lengths ahead of them. A white fire engine and its five-man crew was on point against ghastly 100-foot-high flares with pitch black smoke boiling out of them and rising above the cadre of pumper trucks facing the conflagration. A tall fireman in a white hat sprinted past four of his men as they held their intervals along the heavy canvas fire hose. He came to the man at the end of it as he worked the chrome plated nozzle, aiming its heavy stream of pressurized water at the base of a high wall of advancing flames. One by one, up and down the line, the hoses went dry.

Now, Kathy's white pumper crew was the only one still pumping. Kathy watched the men work together to turn their hose's spray away from the flames and toward the retreating fire crews. The water sputtered out. Kathy watched in horror as the fire gathered strength, rebuilt its heat engine and blasted off.

"The fire's jumping the freeway!" she screamed.

Frank opened his door and stood in time to see a massive solar flare of a flame arch high above all the lanes. Dozens of firemen retreated from it as fast as they could run.

The white pumper crew's captain watched helplessly as enormous tongues of fire, 50 feet over his head, passed fluidly to the other side. He stared up at them, luminous orange under a brown sky. His mouth dropped open at the sight.

My God, they're beautiful, thought the captain, who had driven with his crew all the way from Texas. He had made peace with his love of fire, years ago. He always fought the flames with everything he had—sometimes gambling his very life, but once defeated, he allowed himself a private indulgence. He admired his foe. Loved it even.

The beautiful flaming emissaries quickly accomplished their far-reaching mission. They crossed the wide ocean of air above the freeway, a concrete barrier as wide as a football field. On the other side, they found rich pockets of fuel. The thick brush exploded. New fires immediately began climbing the hillsides south of the Interstate. Frank and Kathy retreated back inside the Suburban.

A deafening roar came suddenly overhead.

"What the hell?"

Frank's question was answered in an instant. An orange C-130 aircraft soared at full throttle a scant 70 feet above the freeway. Its wings waggled as it powered up the furiously burning hill and released a full load of fire retardant. The big plane quickly peeled off to the left. In something like an aerial conga line, the next tanker took its turn, banking sharply from the same direction, dropping 3,000 gallons of water along the fire's edge. Two minutes later, a helicopter swooped down so low the water bucket touched the tongues of the flames. Three hundred gallons of lake water dropped straight down, dousing the fires beneath. The pilot turned his chopper on it's tail and headed again for nearby Lake Jennings. Valiant though these pilots were, with this fire it was like trying to stamp out an anthill with a fly swatter. The fire burned around anything thrown in its path.

Traffic on Interstate 8 was finally allowed to continue once the flames moved uphill. Inside the Suburban, the family sat in silence as Frank drove up the long rutted dirt road which led to Grandma Tammy's ranch.

The Scalari kids had just finished unloading the dogs and the chickens when Tammy came out to the porch looking anguished. Frank and Kathy were preparing to leave.

"Grandma's horse corrals can't hold the goats," said Kathy. "So we're going to leave them with Greg and Joni. They've got a pen."

Tammy stepped forward. "Kathy! *Please!* Don't go back home! The fire's headed straight for your mountain! I saw it on TV! The firemen can't stop it. Those horses aren't worth dying for! *Please* stay here! *Frank!* Talk some sense into her!"

"Mom. No matter what happens, you know I could never leave my horses to die."

"All this for a worthless mustang? You're going to be homeless! Do you want to leave your kids without a mom and dad too?"

"That's *enough!*" roared Frank. "Neo happens to be very valuable to Veronica, and that makes him priceless to me. We *will* bring our horses down safely! That's a promise!"

Frank eased the Suburban and trailer down the rutted dirt road. Kathy poked her head outside the open passenger window and looked back to the house. The Scalari children stood arm in arm, waving goodbye.

JONI'S PRAYER

The air was full of soot and flying embers when Joni spotted Kathy and Frank from her kitchen window. She and the girls came out to watch as Frank slowly backed the horse trailer up our long asphalt driveway. Frank dropped the ramp. He opening the doors at rear of the trailer and the five of them worked together to extract the goats from inside of it. Frank shoved the last reluctant doe into the pen and Joni latched the gate. Kathy and Joni lingered near the pen while Frank secured the trailer.

"This fire is going to get us, Joni, just like you warned me. It's all coming true. It's burning back toward us right now. Our house is going to burn."

Tears traced down Kathy's cheeks. Joni reached out and wiped them with the back of her hand. Ashes fell silently between them, floating down, catching lightly in the women's hair. Joni could see the pain in Kathy's eyes.

"I know things look hopeless for you. We can't do anything now but pray, and I know you don't believe in prayer. I do. The Lord loves hopeless cases, Kathy. I should know — I'm one of them," she said, tapping fingers to the damaged left side of her head, "and now you're one too. All I can do is pray as hard as I know how for you and your property. Nothing is too hard for God. *Nothing!* Not even this terrible firestorm."

"Thanks," said Kathy, politely, "but you haven't seen what I've seen. Even the fire fighters are terrified. This fire's too big. It's too strong. Today on the freeway, we saw firemen running for their lives. No one can save us now, not even your *God*. Tomorrow our mountain will burn and our house will burn will it. Our dream has become a nightmare."

Joni's eyes filled with tears. She gave her anguished friend a hug. She waved goodbye from the gate down at the street as Kathy and Frank headed back to Cuyamaca. As she walked up the long driveway to the house she picked up her silent conversation with the Lord right where it had been left off...

God, Kathy and Frank need a miracle and it's got to be a big one. I've shared You with Kathy for years, but she hasn't believed me. It's got to be big — so big there isn't another explanation besides You! Show them, God!

DANIELLE'S PRAYER

Joni told our girls that the fire was headed to Kathy's house. Juliette's heart ached at the thought of what was going to happen to her friends' farm in the mountains. She had watched the houses of strangers and their children burning down on television for days now, but Julie knew these people. She loved them. She had spent days and weeks of blissful childhood with them, roaming and exploring the place which was soon to be destroyed. Juliette cried.

Danielle listened quietly to her mom as she was told the awful truth of the situation. Afterwards, she wanted to be alone. The 9-year-old ran to the backyard. Joni followed, then stopped. She let her have her space. *God, please help my girls with all of this.*

Danielle reached her swing set, plopped down on a swing and began to rock. She kicked a toe at the ash collecting under her feet and watched her teardrops gently splash-landing on them. She wiped her face and looked up, focusing on a flat piece of brown speckled granite twenty feet away. Danielle was five the day she named it. The big boulder was four inches above the ground and flat as a pancake so she named it Flat Rock. Beyond the far edge of it lay a twenty-foot drop-off with jagged rocks at the bottom. One Christmas, she was riding her brand new two-wheeler too fast on the dirt behind the house when her feet slipped off the pedals. She began to wobble — careening out-of-control and headed straight for Flat Rock. She closed her eyes. Danielle and her bike reached the front lip of the boulder at high speed. The bike flipped wheels over handlebars, cartwheeled off the cliff, and clanged on the rocks below.

The next thing she remembered was opening her eyes in time to watch her doomed bicycle helicopter out of sight. *Somehow*, she had been placed in a sumac tree, ten feet away. Her daddy had seen the whole thing. He told her he had watched helplessly — horrified at the thought of his baby headed for a wheelchair or *worse*, then... POP! Danielle appeared in the little tree, clinging to the trunk. *Maybe God would help my friends like he helped me*, thought Danielle. She cried out through her tears, her voice cracking:

"*God!* Please keep everything just like I remember it! Protect the house, protect the barn, protect the fruit trees and the animals! *Please, Jesus!* Protect the big oak in front of the house with our swing! Keep everything just like it was before the fire!"

Danielle believed that God would answer her prayer. She didn't doubt Him. She had that childlike faith that Jesus says we all must have in the Gospels. That was why her prayer had been so specific. She took every detail to God. She wanted the Scalari's to be spared, and she didn't want to leave anything out. Because she knew God was listening, her prayer could not be vague. Though young, she was already what some would call a "prayer warrior." Her belief in the power of her prayers had been settled four years ago at the tender age of five...

GOD and the REPTILE

"I tell you the truth, anyone who will not receive the kingdom of God like a little child will never enter it."

(Mark 10:15)

MAY 1999

"Daddy, we left Methuselah outside!" said little Danielle, sitting across from me at the wobbly dining table. We were between houses at the time, and living in our motorhome at a rural membership R.V. park. Our pet tortoise, Methuselah, was a favorite of the kids at the park. One afternoon, I fed him his plate of greens and bananas outside the motorhome and got distracted. Ten minutes later, 5-year-old Danielle realized her daddy's mistake, but Methuselah was long gone. The reptile had wandered away into the nearby brush covered hills.

We searched and searched. Danielle made posters with a crayon drawing of Methuselah, but we never saw him again during our long months at the park. Joni and I bought our home in Jamul in June of that year. I drove the motorhome down to it when escrow closed on August 1.

We moved on with our lives without Methuselah. And by we I mean the rest of the family. Danielle never gave up on the tortoise. Months went by yet little Danielle never stopped praying. Each night she asked God to keep Methuselah safe and return him to us. As I listened to her pray for the tortoise night after night for months on end, I began to believe it was time for her to let him go. I was worried that she was setting herself up for terrible disappointment. More troubling, her disappointment involved God. I didn't say anything to her about it, but my heart ached for her every time she faithfully asked God to return Methuselah to us somehow. How would she handle it when she finally understood he was not coming back? To put it mildly, the odds were—well, it was impossible.

October came and went and every night little Danielle continued to pray to the Lord for Methuselah's safety and that he be returned to us. November brought the first cold rain storm, but she didn't think of giving up. She knew Jesus would answer her prayer.

And then... He did.

Thanksgiving was almost here when Joni got a phone call from the R.V. park. Her cell phone number was written on Danielle's faded crayon drawing of the missing pet, which was still posted in the entrance booth window.

"Hello?"

"Hello Joni? I think I've got your tortoise! He walked right off the mountain and into the park," said the ranger, a young man we had befriended during our long stay in the park.

"Is he there with you?" Joni asked.

"Yes, he's in the entrance booth with me in a bucket. He's looking up at me right now!"

"Oh, thank you! We're coming up right away!"

We celebrated that night. God had answered Danielle's persistent prayer. Methuselah was home.

DOOMED   3:45 P.M.

I had Kathy and Frank on my mind as I drove home in my work truck. It had been a miserable, smoky, choking, disastrous day. My head hurt from breathing in the noxious air.

People want electricity and hot water even when the county is burning down. It'll be the same the day the world ends. They'll be calling for service while dodging flaming hail stones.

I knew the Scalari's property was doomed, and there was nothing anyone could do about it. Praying for it didn't seem feasible to me. I didn't want to put God on the spot like that. If He said no, which I was positive He would, then where would I be? *Holding the bag, that's where I'd be. No, I've got a pretty good batting average with answered prayer. No need to mess it up by jumping off the diving board into the spiritual deep end. God closed that end of the pool centuries ago. I hope they got their fire insurance, they're going to need it.*

When I came in through the sliding door, Joni filled me in on the situation.

"Kathy and Frank have been ferrying kids and animals to her Mom's place all day. I just got off the phone with her. They're staying on the mountain tonight."

I looked to the terrible sky to the west of the Cuyamaca Mountains. "They've got to get outta' there! When that fire begins climbing the western slope, it'll burn fast. It'll trap them!"

I flipped on the television news. We watched a story about the latest Cedar Fire victim, The National Football League. For the first time in NFL history a Monday Night Football game had been moved. The San Diego Chargers would play the Miami Dolphins in Tempe, Arizona tonight after the Chargers were forced to abandon San Diego's Qualcomm Stadium because of the choking smoke and the tens of thousands of Cedar Fire refugees camped out there.

I kept flipping. Desperate reports, rising death counts and fiery destruction continued to stream out of every local station. It was a dull, throbbing, 3-day-old toothache that was getting worse. Haggard, hacking reporters shoved their microphones into the faces of tearful homeowners as their homes burned down in front of them. Fire commanders predicted no containment until November. Horrible footage of burned horses being led away to be put down brought all of us to tears.

I shut off the television.

"Neo and Cindy are still up there!" cried Joni.

"But Mom!" Juliette cried, "Veronica's not! And she's the only one who can get Neo to go in the trailer!"

Chapter Five
Escape

Fire burns in front of them, and flames follow after them. Ahead of them the land lies as beautiful as the Garden of Eden. Behind them is nothing but desolation; not one thing escapes.

(Joel 2:3) NLT

Chapter Five

Escape

4:15 P.M.

BACK HOME IN the Cuyamaca Mountains, a panicked search was in progress. "I can't find it. It's here somewhere, but I don't know where," said Kathy.

She was hurriedly searching through a thick pile of papers retrieved from the drawer that served as a catchall for bills, mail, and important documents. She was looking for her copy of the fire insurance agent's inspection report.

"You've got to find it, Kath," Frank urged. He assumed an insurance company would honor their policy, but you never really knew. Especially in the case of a natural disaster. People had been put through the wringer in the past, and he did not want to face the prospect of fighting that battle without so much as a receipt. Worse yet, Frank's $1,700 check still hadn't cleared.

There was more bad news for the Scalaris. Their second trip to Jamul in mid-afternoon delivered only two of their four horses. Neo wasn't one of them. Kathy worked for an hour trying to lead him into the trailer but he wouldn't go. Skip, Alex's small Palomino, and Elyse,Veronica's Arabian mare had gone first instead. An inescapable fire noose was tightening around the base of the Cuyamacas, and as Kathy searched for the insurance papers, she realized there was not enough daylight to make another trip with Neo and Cindy.

Frank and Kathy were exhausted and frightened. They had decided to sleep here at home one last night, or try to do so, but as they walked around their ghost of a house and began saying goodbye to a life within it that they had just barely said hello to, their anxiety and fear grew.

Frank stood by the dining table staring helplessly out the bay window. His mind began playing out catastrophic scenarios:

Most probably the fire will be coming sometime tomorrow from the western slope of Poco Montana. It'll climb to the top, then it'll burn through the forest. The flames will come onto our property out front at the green gate. That field south of us will catch immediately, then the barn will catch fire through the breezeway.

He imagined a swirling shower of red-hot embers blowing in through the 10-foot-high middle of his barn. He could see the straw ignite in a flash. It would be over quickly; his barn would explode from the inside out.

The chicken coop right next to it? 'Fuhgeddaboudit!' The ammonia in all that chicken poop will go up like a 4th of July grand finale. BOOM!

Frank stepped out the door and onto the covered balcony. Three monumental columns of black smoke were furiously making their way toward him. He saw smoke columns coming from the south, the west, and the northwest. His property would soon be surrounded. Once the flames began traveling up the steep western faces of the Cuyamaca Mountains there would be no stopping them. Frank walked part way down the balcony ramp along the windowless south wall of his home and gripped the black iron railing. He stared down at the chain link fence to the spot where he and the surveyor had met to discuss the fence's errant placement.

"That chain link fence is more than five feet off at the southeast pin. It's inside your neighbor's property," the leathery old pro had told him. The two men had stood ten feet from the south wall of the house looking at an oak tree just outside the fence. "We're okay just past this oak, then it veers off. See my corner stake?"

Frank recalled closing an eye to line up his vision, then cutting his line of sight vertically with his right hand in line with the corner stake—its pink ribbon flapping 50 feet to the east.

"Yes, I see what you mean, the fence really jogs off after this tree."

"I just wanted to show you. That fence has been here a long time, just don't build a new one on your neighbor's property."

Now, it was easy to imagine how his home would burn. There, just outside the fence, was a Grim Reaper, standing tall, pointing its bony finger directly at his doomed home. Its outstretched arm stood fifteen feet above the ground and only three feet from the side of his house. The oak tree. Frank never looked up that day in September when he and the surveyor spoke. He wouldn't have noticed the threat it posed today either if it weren't for the onrushing inferno. The trunk of this tree was only 15 feet from the south wall of his house. That was bad enough, but this branch was a fire highway to sure destruction. Add to that the pale yellow carpet of dry foxtails surrounding it and it was a *fait acompli.'*

Fifteen feet. Three feet. Oak tree or not, what's the difference? The heat alone will blow this house sky high.

As a physicist, Frank was fairly well acquainted with the details. When a fire like the Cedar Fire burns, everything is bigger. Some flames reached 200-feet-high yesterday. He and Kathy had seen video of them on a TV news report. Helicopter footage had shown a monstrous wall of advancing flames unlike anything Frank had ever seen. A thermal imaging camera onboard the copter had pegged temperatures above 1,800°F. Houses were seen popping like popcorn —exploding before the flames ever touched them. And Frank knew why. When a tightly closed house with an inside temperature of 85°F is overtaken by a firestorm with temperatures reaching 1,800°F, the 1,715°F difference will be equalized. Something's gotta give and what gives is not the fire, it's the house. Like an overfilled balloon punctured by a sharp needle, once the higher pressure inside a house springs a leak, the temperature *outside* becomes the temperature *inside* and "BOOM!" a house explodes in flames without the fire outside having touched it.

Frank walked down the balcony ramp to ground level behind his house and paused to check his watch. It was 4:25 p.m. The sun had ducked behind the top of Poco Montana, casting its long, late afternoon shadow directly over the barn and the house and all the way back to the long wall of branches. He walked in shade behind the house to the other pile of fuel, the massive stack of logs, the last fleeting rays of sunshine upon them. He turned and crossed the dirt driveway which ran between the two piles and felt sick to his stomach. This was the most volatile mix of kindling: dry pine needles, sawdust, dry weeds and branches. It was a 100-foot-long, five-feet-high powder keg. There was no way to defuse it.

Kathy flung open the screen door at the back porch. "I can't find it!" she cried as she walked toward Frank. "I can't find the fire inspection report!"

Frank shook his head and looked west. The sunlight was gone, replaced by the orange glow of vicious flames destroying lower elevations. "Toast, this place is toast," he muttered.

Frank and Kathy went back into the house and called the kids on Frank's laptop. All four children were visible on the screen as they huddled around Frankie's laptop which sat on Grandma Tammy's kitchen table. Veronica was seated directly in the center.

"Dad? Mom? I can't see you," said Veronica. The screen was scrambled. Suddenly, Kathy and Frank's faces assembled. "Wait...there you are."

"We'll have to make this quick," said Frank, focusing on Veronica's face. "The smoke is jamming the satellite signal. I'm afraid your mom and I are stuck here tonight." Frank saw fear in his daughter's eyes.

"Why, Daddy?" said Veronica. "We need you here with us! Can't you come down now, then go back for the horses in the morning?"

A pixelated image of Frank scrambled in and out as the children watched. "Kids. Listen. Once we leave home the police won't let us come back. The horses will die."

The image on Frank and Kathy's screen fragmented — then reassembled. Anna was sitting on Frankie's lap sucking her thumb. She was crying.

"I want my Mommy and Daddy!"

"Anna! Anna!" cried Kathy.

Anna turned away, hugging Frankie's neck. "Get out of there as soon as you can tomorrow!" said Frankie. "Please?"

Kathy's face filled the screen in front of him. "I'm so proud of all of you. You're such good kids. Alex, I see you honey. Be good."

Later that night, Frank flipped the TV on and watched news reports describing the nearby town of Julian and their own mountain to the south of it as being directly in the path of the firestorm. Kathy was upstairs in the middle bedroom filling plastic bag after plastic bag with clothes for each of her children and she and Frank. She loaded pictures, videos, treasures and keepsakes into the bags, as well. She couldn't take everything. She was too tired to be making these decisions. They'd moved in little more than a month ago, and now she had to make these decisions? With every bag that she loaded her heart broke a little more. The fatigue seemed unbearable.

When she finally finished, eight black plastic bags sat outside the upstairs bedrooms.

"Frank? Will you help me please?" Kathy peered down from the top of the staircase. He had fallen asleep in front of the tube. Grim fire news was still pouring out of it.

Frank roused to his feet and shuffled up the stairs toward the sound of Kathy's voice.

"Frank! I need help!" Kathy repeated.

"I'm coming! Just a minute!"

Frank and Kathy picked up a heavy bag in each hand by the yellow drawstrings and struggled toward the backdoor. Two round trips and eight bags later, the tired couple tried to sleep. They were both physically worn out, but as soon as they crawled beneath the covers they both realized this would be their last night in the home of their dreams. How do you sleep when a monstrous wildfire is blazing toward you? How do you sleep like that? When you don't even know if you're insured? How exactly do you do anything at all under those circumstances?

TUESDAY, OCTOBER 28, 2003

6:50 A.M.

Frank tossed fitfully on their four-poster bed in the early morning light. He was dreaming. It was dark. He looked down from the ceiling into a familiar bedroom. Frank could see a young boy asleep in a maple-framed bed. *My parent's home in Syracuse. That's my bedroom... That's me!*

CRASH! The seven-year-old boy was awakened by the sound of breaking glass. Little Frank bolted upright in his bed. *Someone's in the basement. They've broken into the basement!* The sounds of scuffling footsteps and vile drunken cursing from the basement below his bedroom filled his ears. He was terrified. More than terrified, he was petrified—speechless with fear. He gaped down through a large crack in the floorboards and saw the flashing light of a lit match in the hand of one of the intruders. Little Frank was overtaken by a sense of dread. He let out a scream. The two men in the basement looked up. And they began to grin. The seven-year-old was a lamb for the slaughter. He could hear them laughing at him.

What'll come next? What'll happen to me? the boy wondered. His mom and dad were asleep in their upstairs bedroom—miles away to little Frank. Now he was shivering. He began to hyperventilate. He scrunched his eyes tight. Finally, he managed three words:

"Please help me!"

A man's hand appeared out of the darkness behind the him. It was very large, and it was coming down slowly. It squeezed the boy's shoulder...

"THE FIRE IS COMING. PLEASE EVACUATE THE AREA AS QUICKLY AS POSSIBLE."

Frank bolted up in bed, still wearing yesterday's dirty clothes. The amplified voice had awakened him. Kathy heard it too.

"THE FIRE IS COMING. PLEASE EVACUATE THE AREA AS QUICKLY AS POSSIBLE."

The two of them leapt out of bed and sprinted downstairs to the outside balcony. A green fire truck continued moving north down Engineers Road. The fireman repeated the same message every few seconds through the truck's loud speaker.

The surrounding flames had grown in size throughout the night, becoming more vivid as the fire burned closer and closer to them. Whatever hope they had of the firestorm passing them by was gone now. To the north, to the south, and to the west, uncontrolled flames were converging on their location. Another Santa Ana wind was the only condition that would spare them but that wasn't in the forecast. Frank and Kathy knew their home would burn, and soon.

Frank slumped into a chair near the cafe' table on the balcony. There was so much to do and he was so exhausted. He hadn't slept much and what little sleep he *had* gotten was ruined by that recurring nightmare. *It happened so long ago. Why can't I just forget it?* But he could not forget it. All these decades later, what happened to him in that bedroom was as vivid today as the approaching flames. Something else was bothering him. Something he *had* forgotten. He bolted up in a surge of adrenaline, knocking over the cafe' table.

"I've got gasoline stored in the pump house! I've gotta get it outta there!"

Kathy watched as Frank raced around to the back of the house. He found his green wheelbarrow and rolled it over, stopping outside the door to the power house. He ducked inside. Fuel cans came flying out one after another, clanging into the wheelbarrow until it was full to the brim.

What am I going to do with all this stuff? Frank wondered as he balanced the last red can full of gasoline on top of the others. *Okay, the trash dumpster. It's metal. I'll dump them in there.* He rolled the wheelbarrow over near the tree trunks, piled high against the chain link fence, then he rolled the empty dumpster from its usual location behind the house to where it touched the ends of the stacked logs. He hurriedly threw in the cans of gasoline, kerosene and diesel, then closed the thick plastic lid. If Frank had been thinking clearly, this was the last place he would have rolled the dumpster. He had just rolled a liquid bomb against a massive wooden pile of fuel and both fuel sources were now within fifteen feet of his home.

Kathy came out the back door ten minutes later and found Frank frantically wetting down the jumbled pile of branches behind the house with a weak stream of water from the garden hose. She knew it was pointless. He knew it too. It was *all* pointless. He was kicking ice off the deck of the Titanic.

"Don't you think we better load the horses? It's almost eight."

"Yeah, you're right, I don't think this is going to do any good. They'll just make steam before bursting into flames."

They laughed. It seemed appropriate to laugh in the face of such a hopeless situation. They walked around the north side of the house and downhill toward the apple orchard. The laughter stopped. Black smoke filled the western sky, and at the bottom of the smoke, huge, roaring flames.

"It's time to go, Kath."

Kathy looked grim. "Get the ramp down. I'll get Cindy first."

She ran into the barn and threw a halter on her mare. The Suburban and horse trailer were parked between the barn and the house. Frank dropped the ramp at the rear of it, and Kathy led Cindy out of the barn, directly up the ramp and into the left stall of the trailer. Next up was Neo. Kathy haltered him inside his stall with some difficulty and managed to attach the lead rope, but Kathy was not the one Neo trusted. Veronica was. And as soon as the stall door was opened, the terrified mustang bolted. He jerked the rope out of Kathy's hands and galloped to the far side of the pasture. Kathy and Frank ran after him. The fire was still two miles away but flames were visible. Neo could see them and was panicked.

"He sees the flames!" Kathy yelled, hands waving, fingers spread, as the mustang reared up in front of her.

"He's spooked!" yelled Frank as he ran to his wife's side.

Neo was trying to do what horses always do when confronted by a wildfire—run. When Neo calmed for a moment, Kathy walked up slowly and gently grasped the lead rope. Time after time she led the horse to the edge of the trailer ramp but he would go no further.

Several hours passed as Frank and Kathy struggled to save Neo from being burned alive. Kathy thought about the first time she and Veronica went to see the horse. She remembered feeling sorry for the animal, but once she saw him, she lost all intention of taking him home. He was a crazy and pitiful wreck of a mustang. Veronica had seen *through* Neo's violent spirit and ugly appearance. She had seen something beautiful in him. Something noble in his refusal to give up. Neo had taught Veronica a timeless lesson. Kathy had learned it as well. It was that Veronica's deep and sacrificial love was powerful.

More powerful than the cold, cruel hatred of Neo's human enemy, the cowboy who had tortured him. Veronica had offered her special and precious love to this mustang expecting nothing in return. Her love alone had saved Neo.

Frank and Kathy looked at one another. Veronica was right. She *was* the only one who could get Neo in the trailer. They had to leave and yet how could they possibly explain coming down the mountain without Neo? What would they say?

Susan, a neighbor who was passing by on her way out, spotted Frank and Kathy struggling with the horse in the orchard. Neo kicked up his heels and jumped sideways. Frank pulled on the taut rope with all his might. Susan parked at the green gate out front and hurried to help with the struggle.

"What can I do to help?" she asked.

"I don't know," Kathy replied.

Frank yanked down on the rope again. "I don't know either, but if we don't get him into the trailer soon we're going to have to just let him run free."

"We can't do that!" Kathy snapped.

"What are we supposed to do? It's coming, Kath! The fire is coming!"

"I know! I know! Let's try one more time!"

Frank looked at Neo. "Here," he said. "Let me try."

He began talking to the horse. Gently. Very gently. Frank's heart was pounding. All he could think of was Veronica. She would be devastated. Wild thoughts went through his mind. Maybe she would refuse to talk to him again.

Concentrate, he told himself. *Focus.*

He began telling Neo what a good horse he was. Then he gave the little mustang some slack. Neo stood listening, nostrils flaring, then, slowly, patiently, Frank turned his back to the horse. He began to walk while clicking his tongue. Neo followed. Finally, Frank was able to coax the mustang just past the barn and onto the bottom of the trailer ramp...

1:00 P.M.

The phone was ringing. Joni saw the caller I.D. and put it to her ear: "Greg?"

95

"Joni. I'm parked at a spot where I can see Cuyamaca. All I can see is a plume of black boiling smoke! It must be 20,000 feet high! The fire's climbing the front of their mountain. Have you heard from them today?"

"No! They must still be up there!"

"I hope not. There's no hope for that mountain. Call me if you hear from them." I hung up and stared at the burning mountain. *Get out of there, Frank!*

1:01 P.M.

Kathy and Susan watched in amazement as Neo willingly began following Frank up the trailer ramp.

"I didn't know Frank had such a way with horses," said Susan.

"Me either. Look at that."

Frank entered the trailer stall a few feet ahead of Neo.

"Atta boy," Frank said gently. "Come on, Neo. Almost there. Come on."

Frank imagined Veronica's smiling face as the mustang poked his head into the trailer stall. He was going to bring Neo back to her. At least something important was going to be salvaged.

But there was something no one noticed. Out of the hazy smoke came the same light green fire truck that had warned the neighborhood early that morning.

Suddenly the fireman shouted over the loudspeaker again, this time in an angry voice:

"*ATTENTION! THIS IS YOUR LAST WARNING!*"

At this, Neo jumped, springing sideways off the ramp, ripping the rope through Frank's bare hands. He felt its hot friction burning his palms. Neo galloped out the gate toward Engineers Road. That was it.

"*LEAVE THE HORSE! GET OUT NOW!*" screamed the fireman.

Frank hung his head. He took a deep breath. It had all come to nothing. He closed his eyes.

Kathy ran out the gate after Neo onto Engineers Road without even thinking about what she would do. All she knew was that she couldn't give up. Neo galloped one direction, then the other, but fire was coming from all sides. Kathy stood in the middle of the road, arms outstretched, watching as the mustang made his turn 100 yards away. Frank watched helplessly as Neo charged in his wife's direction. She began frantically waving her arms. Frank ran toward her, but too late.

The sound of hoof beats on the asphalt filled Kathy's ears. She could see fear in Neo's eyes, the whites of them flashing to and fro, his head thrashing side to side. She held her ground though. Neo wasn't stopping, and she wasn't backing down.

Neo accelerated toward her from 75 yards away. She raised her hands high over her head and closed her eyes tight. "Whoa! Neo! Whoa!" she commanded.

The hoof beats became deafening.

"Neo! Whoa!"

The hoofs broke rhythm, clattering and skidding out-of-control. She opened her eyes in time to see the 1000 pound horse sliding toward her from ten feet away. Kathy felt one of the horse's hot wet nostrils slap against her face. She locked her arms around his neck in a desperate bear hug and rode out the slide. When the dust cleared, Kathy found that she was relatively unhurt, other than a scrape on the forehead from the buckle of the mustang's halter. Neo had scrabbled back up onto his hooves. Kathy got to her feet too. She took a firm hold on the lead rope and jerked it down quickly to refocus Neo's attention. She walked him back to Frank who stood there stunned. He had never seen a more determined look on his wife's face.

"I'm going to lead him out on foot until he can't see the fire," Kathy said. "Just drive a little behind me."

Frank closed the trailer ramp and slid into the driver's seat. Susan stood watching as Kathy walked the wet and frothy mustang past the passenger's side window of the SUV. As Frank followed behind on Engineers Road, Kathy began to run. Neo trotted alongside her on the asphalt as they began a steady incline up the first long switchback. Smoke from the advancing flames to the west choked Kathy as she continued the uphill run. By the third turn, she began hacking and coughing. She slowed to a walk. She couldn't run anymore. Frank brought the Suburban and trailer to a stop just ahead of her. She walked the horse up to the open window of the front passenger door.

"I can't keep going, Frank," she panted. But she had an idea. She stepped up onto the running board beside the front passenger's door and grabbed the handhold inside the open window. "Just go slowly."

Frank eased his foot on the accelerator. This really would be their last chance.

Neo trotted beside Kathy as she perched precariously on the sideboard while gripping the lead rope in one hand and the handhold inside the SUV in the other. Making matters worse, fire engines passed in the opposite direction, many of them yelling for her to let the horse go.

Good luck with that boys, Frank thought to himself.

Her family was about to lose everything. But not Neo. She was not about to give up. Traffic was piling up behind them, yet these fellow Cuyamaca refugees who were also evacuating their doomed homes wanted to do nothing but help. Halfway up the mountain, Kathy leaned into the open front passenger window of the Suburban. "Let's see if he'll go into the trailer."

The neighbors stopped behind them, getting out of their vehicles and gathering behind the trailer to try to help. Frank dropped the ramp while Kathy led Neo around to the rear. She trudged up the ramp and pulled firmly on the lead rope. Neo strained against it. The small crowd of motorists pushed on the mustang's rump. Cindy neighed loudly from the other side, bobbing her head, crashing hard on the stall wall. A man in a blue pickup suggested they try again at the top of the ascent.

"We won't leave you until your horse is in the trailer!" said Susan, who was committed to seeing at least one happy ending in the midst of such sorrow.

Frank and the man with the blue truck lifted the trailer ramp and secured it. Emotion rose in Frank's throat as he scanned the crowd of his neighbors.

"Thank you," he told them.

The drivers took their places and Kathy climbed back on the running board with Neo alongside. The improvised procession began moving again, the tall blonde woman and the small brown horse at the front of it. Mile after mile they climbed in the smoky gloom, the growing line of traffic behind them. Every car's headlights were on. It looked like a funeral procession. At the top, where the fire wasn't visible, Frank pulled off the road again. The growing crowd of neighbors pulled off behind them. Newcomers at the back of the line did so as well, unsure of why, but too curious to drive by without knowing. Neo was now too tired to put up a fight. He turned his head and stared at the audience that had gathered in a semicircle behind him. Frank and his helper dropped the trailer ramp. The evacuees watched quietly as Kathy walked the tired mustang up the ramp and into the trailer. She unlatched the rope from his halter then broke into a broad smile. The crowd let out a shout and began clapping. Frank and his helper secured the ramp while the celebration continued.

WAAAAAA! WAAA! WAAAAA! A white pumper truck's captain blared a right-of-way warning. The startled crowd broke up and quickly dispersed into their cars and trucks. Every vehicle was filled to capacity with pictures, treasured small items and clothes.

Being out of immediate danger, Kathy closed her eyes. Frank drove by Lake Cuyamaca. She pictured her house, her back porch, and she began to list all the things they'd left behind. She gasped.

"Our clothes! We left everything sitting in plastic bags on the back porch!"

Frank looked down at his torn shirt, filthy jeans, and worn out boots. "We can't go back," he said flatly.

Kathy sighed. Frank turned west onto I-8. Kathy heard a chirp from her cell phone. It had found service. The phone began to ring.

"Kathy? Are you OK?" It was Joni.

"Oh my God! It's scary up here, Joni!" Kathy scanned the terrifying scene north of the Interstate. "Everywhere I look I see fire. We're going to be homeless. All the firemen have gone to Julian."

"You can stay here with us," Joni offered. "Don't give up. I've been praying. Miracles happen."

"Where is this God of yours now?" Kathy asked. "Thousands of people have already lost their homes!"

Frank rolled his eyes.

Kathy retreated. "I'm sorry Joni, I'm just really upset."

"Were you able to get your clothes and pictures out at least?"

"I packed all our clothes and pictures in plastic bags, but then Neo ran away and I forgot them. The bags are still sitting on the back porch."

"Oh. I'm so sorry. What happened to Neo? Is he... Is he with you?"

"Yeah. After I ran him up the mountain. You wouldn't believe what happened. I'm tired, Joni. Too tired to cry." The tears began to flow anyway. "I can't talk right now," she apologized, and covered her mouth with a shaky hand. "Bye."

POCO MONTANA   3:00 P.M.

Pine Hills Fire Station sat facing Boulder Creek Road just across from the steep western face of Poco Montana. Around the station was a freshly bulldozed ring of bare dirt, 150 feet wide. A D-9 bulldozer sat idling in the freshly scraped field. Jesse, a 22-year-old newly qualified fire equipment operator, was standing in that field with his back to the 'dozer, staring up at the imposingly steep peak in front of him. Thick with brush and pines, Poco Montana was a "dead man walking" in his thinking. One bulldozer, one engine, and a hand crew was all they had at this location. A parade of fire engines and their crews had driven through earlier today on their way to staging areas near Julian, fifteen miles to the northeast. Now, Jesse and his crew were on their own to do what they could, then make it out alive.

Jesse turned on his heels and made tracks in the soft dirt straight for the D-9, a rig called the Big Cat. He climbed the metal foot rungs and knocked on the cab door. The D-9's operator, Tug, popped open the dark tinted cab window. Toby Keith was blaring. Tug cut Toby down to a whisper. Jesse and Tug looked at one another knowing things were bad. Tug's prized cap with "Caterpillar" in bold face above a tiny yellow D-9 sat low on his brow. He was ready for business.

At 34, Tug had worked many wildfires over the last fifteen years. The hours were long, the danger was high, but the money was good. CDF checks never bounced. He could see the youthfulness in Jesse's face, but he didn't hold it against him. He waited to hear what was on this young fire pup's mind.

"You see that face right there, that's Poco Montana," Jesse said. "I don't want to put you or us up on that thing, we've gotta let it burn. Those houses behind it too. We get caught back in there and there's not much chance of coming out alive."

Five years ago a fire commander had become aggressive and reckless with Tug and his crew of dozer operators. Six of them were cutting firebreaks above a fast moving fire on a mountain much like Poco Montana when the fire quickly surrounded them. They survived by carving themselves a clearing and bunching the dozers in a circle, blades up and facing out. The men lay face down in the center of the dozers under reflective fire blankets, faces in the dirt, while the fire passed over them. The youngster had just earned Tug's respect though it was clear he didn't have a plan in the world beyond not heading up Poco Montana.

"OK, I'll head down Boulder Creek way, and start cutting lines across the swale. We've got a couple of ways out if it starts coming at us." Then Tug threw the kid a bone. "Is that what you had in mind?"

Jesse smiled in relief: "Yes sir! That's just what I was thinking."

Tug loaded his lower lip with a pinch of tobacco and cranked Toby up again. Jesse gave a thumbs up and hopped down off the bottom rung. The cab window clicked shut. Jesse walked a few feet away and watched the Big Cat spin around on one track, raise its blade and begin clanking its way southeast on Boulder Creek Road.

Neither Tug in his D-9, nor Jesse and his crew would ever cut a firebreak in Cuyamaca Woods. The Scalari's home, and the homes of their neighbors, had been left to burn.

JULIAN

JOHN GASTALDO UNION/TRIBUNE   BACKBURN RACES AWAY

Chapter Six
Inside The Furnace

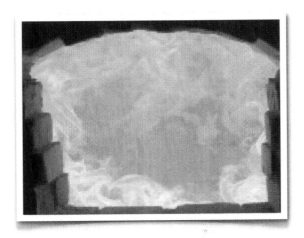

The difference between a Miracle and a Fact is exactly the difference between a mermaid and a seal. It could not be expressed better.

MARK TWAIN

Chapter Six
Inside The Furnace

5:30 P.M.

I SAT AROUND the supper table with Joni and the girls and began preparing them for the worst. "It doesn't matter if we don't have wind down here," I explained. "That firestorm creates its *own* wind. Nothing can stop the fire now, except lack of fuel, but there's plenty of fuel everywhere on their mountain. Remember those big piles of wood near the house? They've got no chance."

Danielle had a surprise for her pessimistic father.

"Me and Mom prayed for their property, Dad," she stated. "I asked God to keep it just like I remember it. I asked Him to keep it just like it was before the fire."

I thought of Danielle's powerful prayers for Methuselah, the tortoise who was at that moment hibernating in a box in Danielle's closet. I had believed recovering Methuselah was impossible. And yet, against all odds Methuselah was returned to us. Danielle had

105

never stopped believing God would bring Methuselah back.

"I asked God to show them who He is," Joni added. "To give Kathy and Frank a miracle that they can't possibly explain."

I reflected back on what I had seen just a month earlier on Bellows Beach on Oahu. A vision played over and over in my mind. It was the sight of my wife jamming her hands into a directed place in the seabed. *What kind of woman does that? What kind of woman walks into the ocean praying, gets directions from God, follows them, then finds what she was praying for buried in the coral sand? So I guess God knows everything. Even where our lost sunglasses are buried? Imagine that.*

Their faith gave me pause, but it did no more than that. The Miracle of Methuselah was impressive, no doubt. The Maui Jim's were a stunner. But they were no Cedar Fire. This was different. This wasn't about long odds. This was about something that was simply impossible. *What incredible faith,* I thought. *But this time, the two of them have bitten off more than God is willing to chew.*

One mile east of us at Tammy's ranch, Frank had just returned from town with bags full of fish tacos, a San Diego favorite. The Scarlari family was together again. They celebrated. Veronica took a bite of taco, sat it down on her plate and disappeared out the front screen door.

Kathy smiled, knowing exactly where her daughter was headed. She stepped out onto the front porch into smoky twilight and listened. Between the crickets, she could faintly hear Veronica's voice in the distance, speaking soft loving words. She was with Neo. Kathy sighed deeply. At least one thing had gone right. At least the animal Veronica loved the most was safely returned to her. A rooster crowed. Kathy's eyes widened. She and Frank had forgotten something *besides* the bags full of pictures and clothes. A chicken. *Chocolate! We forgot to look for Chocolate!*

Veronica placed another carrot on her open palm and offered it to Neo. He tickled her palm with his chin whiskers and gently grabbed it. As he chomped on it, Veronica looked up to the distant sky and saw huge orange flames undulating in slow motion, traveling uphill over her mountains, 60 miles away. She focused again on Neo. The 13-year-old girl reached up and gently hugged his neck. "You're okay now, pretty boy. I'm here. Nobody wants to hurt you. You're safe."

Neo closed his eyes. He exhaled.

BLOW TORCH   8:00 P.M.

One thousand and three hundred feet above the abandoned Pine Hills Fire Station the peak of Poco Montana was roaring with furious fire. Unchecked by man or nature, the merciless consumption ebbed, then flowed, then exploded in an instant, a rich pocket of dead pines combusting like a Kuwait oil well fire. An hour earlier, flames the size of skyscrapers sprinted up the sharp western face all the way to the top. Now the firestorm was burning around both the northern and southern shoulders of the mountain. The rolling and crackling sounded like a million fireplace fires released from their controlled confines, free to rampage, to probe blindly for the fuel that kept it alive. Punctuating that sound was the terrific snap and crash of enormous pines as the inferno leapt uphill, roasting everything in its path. Deer were overtaken at a full run.

Cuyamaca Woods below was fully illuminated by Poco Montana, a gigantic blow torch of a mountain, though only two pairs of eyes were there to see it.

In a hidden corner of the Scalari's barn, Chocolate, Veronica's missing black hen, came out of hiding. The bright light from the approaching flames made the little chicken believe a new day had begun and so she set about her daylight activities. She pecked and scratched for bugs in the large field of dry grass between the barn and the house. The little hen clawed at a rock, overturned it and found what she was looking for — a nest of earwigs.

Chocolate was quite excited... *Eck-eck-eck-eck*

The earwigs squirmed in the light of a fire far brighter than a full moon. Chocolate began eagerly pecking and skewering insect after insect, filling her belly with the black, squirming, pincher bugs. The empty field of high weeds outside the southern property line was in flames now. Chocolate seemed unbothered.

The second witness was a human one.

Tom Wilby, the neighbor to the south of Frank and Kathy, was still at home. He had put himself at great risk in an attempt to save his home and barn. Tom had spent the last eight hours soaking his house and the area surrounding it with 5,000 gallons of water from his now-empty water tank. He reached down to shut off the remaining trickle from the spigot and saw rapidly approaching flames reflected in a mosaic of water pockets on the ground. He mucked his way over the muddy bog to the front porch landing. He stepped up quickly and slipped, splash-landing on his behind, directly beneath the rain gutter down-spout. Water flooded onto his face. He sat up straight, wiped the water from his eyes with the inside of his forearm, then gazed northeast toward the Scalari's house, 1,000 feet away.

The log stack was burning. Twelve cords worth of it, a few feet from the rear porch of Kathy and Frank's home. Huge, white-hot and intense, the flames were staggering in height. They dwarfed the surrounding fires by a measure of three to one. Hundreds of four-foot-long, twenty-inch diameter pine tree trunks were burning in unison creating a 2,000°F crematorium. Nothing in the surrounding area was burning as hot as this massive collection of pine tree trunks. The constant roar from it sounded like 50 hot air balloons firing their propane burners all at once. The chain link fence glowed red hot, melting down to a gnarly goo.

Tom took a seat on his teakwood porch swing just as the gasoline and everything else in the dumpster at the front of the logs blew to the heavens. His lower jaw fell slack at the sight, purple and yellow fireballs rolling up to the soot-filled sky. Then came the sound of the explosions as each fuel container gave way.

BOOM!... BOOM!..BOOM!....B O O M!

He heard whistling like a tea kettle coming from the burnt orange ceiling high above his house. He stepped off the porch and looked up. A small flaming comet arced high over his place, a long tail of fluttering yellow flame behind it. One of Frank's fuel cans was rocketing its way back to earth. CANG! WHRRRR! The can bounced and rolled down the asphalt of Engineers Road, 200 feet away.

Back at the Scalari's, the intruding oak tree near the south side of the house and outside the melting chain link fence was completely engulfed in flames. The intruding branch, as well. Fifteen feet east of this oak sat the metal dumpster, still burning, and the white hot, rocket-motor temperatures of the burning logs stacked next to it. Ash-colored oak leaves shot skyward beyond the boundary in a shower of embers, cascading down to ground already thick with lifeless remnants. The branches, stacked all along the east line behind the house, were burning in an incredible way. Flames outside of the invisible boundary were making quick work of the pine needles, sawdust, and kindling, blackening the ground beyond the manmade margin. The branches themselves, although on fire, were not blackening.

Tom didn't know exactly what was burning with so much intensity over at Frank's place, but the flaming mortar shell of a gas can had focused his mind. "It's time to go!"

He entered his home for the last time and picked up the landline and punched a number into the phone.

Sharon, his wife, had driven off the mountain and down to a friend's house in mid-afternoon. Tom wouldn't leave. She had been desperate to hear from him for hours. The phone rang. Sharon saw the caller I.D. "Tom? Tom?"

"Yes, Sharon, it's me. I've done all I can. I'm getting out of —" The line went dead, burned through.

Tom took an ill-advised few moments to have a final look around. He said goodbye to his old friend, this house, this young man's dream become this old man's nightmare. The house was speaking to him. With each glance the memories poured out. The driftwood fireplace mantle where his children hung Christmas stockings when they were small. *That Christmas Eve, it rained hard, but when the kids woke up the rain had turned to snow.* His kitchen, his trusted pots and pans still hanging at the ready. *Our 25th wedding anniversary. I made Veal Scaloppini for Sharon, with shiitake mushroom sauce and small red potatoes.* The carved wooden staircase. At the bottom, a cheerful yellow sign read: KEEP YOUR TIPS UP. *I borrowed it on that Tahoe ski vacation in '86.*

The house was nothing but a phantom now, dematerializing before his eyes. Still here but already gone, a memory that still stood for the moment. He hurried out the front door, checked his soaked pants for his wallet and car keys, then locked the door behind him. Tom sprinted for his car on the dirt road out front. He glanced at the barn, one hundred feet north of him. Terrible fire surrounded it.

WUMP!

His barn exploded in front of him with a deafening crack of spontaneous ignition. Hot shards of thin metal skin came glittering toward him as he ducked behind his car.

"Oh no! *Oh no!*" he shouted, his anguished voice cracking. He had waited too long. The wildfire was upon him.

Tom's wife and friends were praying for him, asking God to spare his life. They begged for him to make it out safely.

Tom held his breath against the superheated blast of toxic gases from the combusting contents of the disintegrating barn. He focused only upon the driver's side door handle of his car. He realized that to breathe now would be to pass out and die. He visualized his grisly remains lying beside the burned out shell of his car, his beloved wife horrified at finding him like that. He screamed inside his head: *Open the door Tom! C'mon! Grab the handle!*

Tom grabbed the hot handle of his driver's side door. "*Locked!*"

He pulled his keys out of his right front trouser pocket. He dropped them. The scorching heat of the fire's poisonous breath surrounded him. There was no choice. He had to get down on his hands and knees and scour the hot embers and dirt for his keys. He found them, jumped to his feet, unlocked the door and slid in. There was still good air remaining inside the car. He took a deep breath as he turned the ignition key. *Nothing.*

"Come on now! I gotta get outta here!" Tom stepped on the brake pedal and wiggled the steering wheel. He tried the key again. DRRRRRUM! The engine came to life and he slammed it into drive. He glanced back at his home one last time. White steam rose from his wet roof like a house-sized pressure cooker, which in fact, it was. His home exploded and burned to the ground in the time it took him to drive the flaming gauntlet to Lake Cuyamaca. Tom escaped shaken but unharmed.

Outside of the Scalari's western property line, three fronts of the same fire had converged. An hour ago, flames had burned up and around the southern face of Poco Montana, catching and burning the open field of high grass to the south of their property. The racing fire had sprinted across the field to the stacked tree trunks, the dumpster, the branch stack, and farther south, Tom's barn and home. Now, fire from around the mountain's northern and southern shoulders came together along the Scalari's western boundary. Enormous, jagged and merciless, this flaming, multi-headed hydra was rapidly destroying whatever forest Poco Montana had left.

Frank and Kathy's neighbors to the north had been out of town. The Cedar Fire was paying a devastating visit. No one was there to see or hear the metal barn in the seconds before it exploded, its weather vane spinning clockwise, then counterclockwise in erratic circles, its contents igniting in a flash of light and thunderous clap.

Fierce winds blew in many directions at the same time, streaming to various locations of white-hot flames. Magnitude 10 firestorms like the Cedar Fire take on almost demonic characteristics. They are powerful beyond imagining and are capable of producing strange and terrifying flames that act like revolving, fire-breathing monsters. One such entity stood swirling directly in front of the northern neighbor's home, howling like a freight train, its vivid, flaming vortex bending low, white-hot inside the swirl, blue and orange at the spinning outer walls. It resembled, more than anything else, a flaming genie released from the bowels of hell. The faster it spun, the bigger it grew, until the wicked pillar of fire was fully 20 feet wide and 200 feet high.

A tree isn't up to the contest. Nor a house. Nor even a mountain. The Scalari's neighbor's house was consumed in short order. Every window shattered. The house disintegrated and burned to the ground in minutes. The fiery cyclone traveled on, still hungry, a glutton zigzagging its way uphill to the east, pushed and pulled by the firestorm's wind, hop-scotching and fire-starting all the way to Lake Cuyamaca.

In the middle of this havoc, a strange sight was visible though no one was there to see it. A wooden stool was on fire—or was it? The seat of the stool was partially protruding through the old hog-wire fence on the western boundary and hanging into the easement. Before the fire started the previous Saturday, a 50-mile-per-hour wind gust slammed this stool through the hog-wire. It stuck right where the fence caught it, legs-side-in and seat-side-out. Now, smoke billowed from the burning, blackening seat of the stool, but for some reason the legs had not caught fire.

Chocolate, meanwhile, sat nestled on the front balcony up at the house. Inside her tiny brain she was motivated by only one thing: her empty stomach. She mechanically cocked her head at the sight of the horrific holocaust around her and knew no fear of it. The black hen turned to face the big oak tree in front of her. The swing hung deathly still. There was no wind. She waddled along the wood plank floor, bobbing her head and flapping her wings. The young pullet spread her feathery limbs and flew down to the ground in search of earwigs again. She rounded the corner between the house and the 150-foot-high flames actively cremating the stack of tree trunks. The bugs were easy for her to spot. The fire's light made it as bright as day. Not a breath of wind was moving even the smallest leaf.

The secret things belong to the LORD our God, but the things revealed belong to us and to our children forever...

(Deut. 29:29)

SECRETS 2:07 A.M.

The fuel in Cuyamaca Woods now exhausted, the flames burned uphill toward the summit. Two miles to the south, a slower, southern front of the Cedar Fire reached the western slope of the ancient pine forest that Veronica and Frankie had ridden through a month and a half ago. At the bottom, in the stream the Indians called Ah-ha-'Mi-Ah-ha,' orange flames reflected onto a waterfall as it cascaded down to the place in the brook where the brother and sister had watched the mother mule deer and her fawn.

The beautiful mysteries within the dark forest were brightly revealed in the harsh light of luminous destruction, stripped naked in the unsparing glare of catastrophe. Once set ablaze, these irreplaceable, towering pines were sent sprawling like bowling pins in a flood of encompassing blazes. The fire burned away everything magical, everything mystical, revealing all the mountain's secrets. Huge oaks in a grove at southern end of the carbonizing forest were on fire now. Indian grinding holes in the granite beneath them were filled with glowing embers.

Below Cuyamaca Peak to the south, on the high plateau where the Indian village of Rabbit House once thrived, a huge ocean of fire licked at the base of 2,000 foot cliffs. To the north of it, Middle Peak was fully engulfed Not a tree upon it would survive.

4:07 A.M.

From a hidden thicket within earshot of the icy brook, a doe watched the progress of the onrushing flames, her fawn tucked beneath her. Only the eyes, ears and nose of the little buck were visible from his cozy refuge behind his mother's neck. The doe peered out at the unusual light of the great fire. The deer did not have the ability to make sense of the onrushing disaster. The closer it came, the smaller she made herself. Finally, any fear she had of being seen was overtaken by the brutal heat that overcame her and her little buck. She had no choice but to flee. Every animal, large and small, ran in only one direction. *Away.*

Nearby, a mountain lion was running for *her* life. Prey and predator ran side by side. Does and fawns, mountain lions and cubs, foxes and rabbits were in a race against scorching death. Most all of them lost.

Hundreds of square miles would burn in the dark hours of Wednesday morning.

Ah-ha'-Mi-Ah-ha' (Water Colder Water)
Early Wednesday, October 29th, 2003

200-FOOT-HIGH VORTEX OF FLAME

JOHN GASTALDO / UNION-TRIBUNE

JOHN GASTALDO/Union-Tribune

Lake Cuyamaca, Wednesday morning, October 29, 2003

Chapter Seven
Uncovered

Nothing in all creation is hidden from God's sight. Everything is uncovered and laid bare before the eyes of him to whom we must give account.

(Hebrews 4:13)

Chapter Seven
Uncovered

WEDNESDAY, OCTOBER 29, 2003   **9:25 A.M.**

"DENIED? WHAT DO you mean our policy is denied?" Kathy shook with anger while she spoke with the fire insurance company representative on the phone.

"Your agent was at my home two weeks ago!" she screamed, trembling as she slumped into her mother's overstuffed blue couch. As she listened, tears slipped down her cheeks. "Yes, I got a receipt from him."

Anna climbed onto the couch and snuggled next to her Mama. Kathy wrapped her arm around her little one and squeezed.

"You don't show any record of the policy going into effect?" She rose to her feet and began to pace. "But he passed us! He told both of us that we were insured! Do I have it? No! It's at my house!" Those last four words tore Kathy wide open. She threw the phone down.

"*What* house? I don't *have* a house anymore!"

Kathy stormed out the front door into hazy sunlight and ambled around to behind the house. She lurched to a stop. Above her, a massive mushroom shaped tower of smoke obscured the distant mountain where her home had stood just yesterday afternoon. The steep foothill in front of her looked more ominous than ever. Hundreds of boulders, many of them as large as a house and weighing hundreds of tons, sat perched 500 feet up and a half mile back. When her mother bought this place, years ago, Kathy had cast a wary eye on this mountain. Today, it seemed to her a perfect metaphor for life. The crushing boulders at rest within their precarious places would not always remain so. Catastrophe would come to the very spot where she stood.

Some day, an earthquake, or a landslide during a heavy rain will bring those boulders down, she thought.

"No house! No fire insurance! A mortgage on what? A chimney?" Her voice echoed off the quiet hills. She stared at one particularly huge gravity defying rock *way* up at the top.

The Cedar Fire had stripped away the pride and the fiction in Kathy's perception of what she could control and what she could not. She wasn't ready to surrender, but the battle was already lost. Her future was up in smoke along with her uninsured home.

Why didn't Frank see this coming? He knew that mountain was ready to burn. He should've just told me no!

Kathy felt sick to her stomach. Her knees began to buckle. Fear and regret filled her heart. "There's nothing left! The house is gone and it's my fault! I'm the one that found it!"

She closed her eyes and visualized that house-sized boulder, 'way up at the top, beginning to tumble down toward her. *I couldn't find that receipt! Good mothers don't screw up. I screwed up!* She imagined it smacking off another one and launching straight up into the air, one hundred feet above her. The boulder grew larger and larger as it fell, casting its cooling shadow directly over her. Suddenly, Kathy felt very small. Very powerless. It felt good. She let out a laugh. Then she heard one of her children.

Mom? Are you okay?" asked 9-year-old Alex.

Kathy opened her eyes. She focused again on the far away boulders still in their places. Her children were counting on her. She resolved to not let them down. "Yes, honey. I'm okay. I'm just upset, you know? Someday those rocks are gonna fall, Alex. But not today. We're all right today."

Frank overslept, exhausted from yesterday's harsh struggles. When he awoke, he glanced at his watch and sprang out of an unfamiliar bed. "Whose bed? Oh crap."

Frank imagined his and Kathy's king-sized four-poster as it looked this morning, fallen down through the burned out second story floorboards, the mattress reduced to a charred box of empty metal springs.

I never wanted that place. She just had to have it. I gave her what she wanted. Now this. Great. Just great.

He mumbled good morning to his mother-in-law as they passed in the hall, then dragged himself to the bathroom for a hot shower. Afterwards, Frank put on the same filthy clothes he had just taken off—the only clothes he had to his name. He shuffled into the kitchen and nuked some hours old coffee. Kathy cooked him some eggs. A hard deadline for his company's proprietary software project loomed over Frank in mid-November, just two weeks ahead. His family's personal tragedy would not change that fact.

"I'm going to be working all day on my laptop." Frank said flatly.

"But we need to get some clothes, Frank. When will you come shopping with me?"

He imagined the two of them walking through the Fashion Valley Mall, dressed as they were, looking like sharecroppers out of the dust bowl. He had to laugh. "We'll look like Ma and Pa Kettle. Let me work today and we'll go later on tonight, okay?"

Veronica and Anna walked out to Grandma's tack room which was now a makeshift chicken coop. Ten hens and two roosters paced excitedly along the floor of the weather-beaten shack, their heads moving in freeze-frame rhythm, bobbing and tilting as they watched Veronica dip her scoop into a bag of chicken feed. Anna scolded some of the big chickens for stepping on the smaller ones, then she froze in place remembering. "I miss Choc-lette."

Veronica held the full scoop high, shaking it evenly over the mob of squawking poultry, but her thoughts were on the only chicken she really cared about. "I do too, Anna." She gave her little sister a hug.

123

Later that afternoon, Kathy brought Frank a tray of food. She found him hunched over his laptop, ear buds in place and Metallica cranking.

"Oh. Thanks," he said. "I...*uh*... I need to show you something." Frank clicked back to a website — the California Department of Forestry's list of destroyed homes. He scanned down the list with his index finger and stopped two-thirds of the way down.

Kathy read the numbers of the address one at a time, carefully, hoping Frank had seen it wrong. "Oh no! Oh *no!*"

She had known this was what was going to happen. Frank had known. But now to see it in black and white. To read the official pronouncement — their home's obituary. Somehow that made it more real. Frank put his arms around her and hugged her tight. The house was gone.

4:15 P.M.

Kathy drove her children over to our place around four. As Joni and I sat listening to Kathy's heartbreak, we felt helpless.

"Frank just found our address on the Internet. We're *homeless!*"

"At least you're insured," I said, trying to find a bright side.

"Those bastards! I couldn't find the receipt. Now they claim to show no record of our new policy going into effect! We're going to have to sue them over it and we probably won't win, unless they cashed the check. It still hasn't cleared!"

Their house is gone, and so is Cuyamaca. What a nightmare for them, I thought. *The timing of them buying that place couldn't have been worse. No insurance. Where will they live?*

Joni listened attentively to Kathy's story, but it confused her. God had never ignored her urgent prayers before, but the confirmation of their home's destruction was final. For days we had watched news about the fire on television. Watched as firemen swept through neighborhoods with spray paint and yellow tape, cordoning off, then spray painting numbers and warnings on thousands of condemned, uninhabitable homes, and not once were they wrong with their pronouncements. It was over.

"I'm so sorry," said Joni.

AFTERMATH

During the Scalari family's four day stay in Jamul, the Cedar Fire was finally contained after burning its way around Lake Cuyamaca, then uphill to the summit overlooking the Borrego Desert. Having confronted the desert, the worst fire in California history finally and simply ran out of fuel. A few homes here and there were somehow spared in areas overrun by the flames. One house in Crest simply didn't burn, though everything right up to the house did. There was heat damage, but the house still stood. Otherwise, the destruction was mind-boggling. The Cedar Fire killed 15 people. There were 113 injures. The estimated cost of fighting the fire was put at 31 million dollars. It had spread at a rate of 3,600 acres per hour in the first 36 hours. At one point, it spread an unbelievable 40,000 acres in a single hour.

When the total was finally tallied, 2,232 homes were destroyed. The Scalari's house was listed as one of them and their insurance company was denying that they had a policy. All that remained was for Kathy and Frank to go and see the devastation with their own eyes.

THE FUNERAL

NOVEMBER 1, 2003   7:30 A.M.

Frank stared straight ahead at the freeway as he drove Kathy up to Cuyamaca for the first time since fleeing the flames last Tuesday. The silence between them was broken only by the Suburban's heater fan and the engine surging on the steady incline. They were sharing the same dreadful anticipation, both of them alone in their thoughts. It was a trip to the funeral home to see a recently departed loved one, a life that was no more. *Their* life.

How will it look? Frank wondered. *Rest assured, it won't look good.*

The ground on both sides of the Interstate was scorched black. This trip would confirm what they already knew, but they needed to see with it their own eyes. And they needed to scour the remains of

125

their uninsured home for whatever small remnants of their former life they might find.

There'll be no power, no water, no house, thought Frank. *The barn will be gone, blown apart, none of the walls standing. Charcoaled rectangles where stalls used to be. The chicken coop will be totally gone. The apple orchard burned to the ground. The trees? Black trunks and black branches. The big oak tree's trunk will be thick with soot. The swing will be gone.*

The house. Frank imagined Kathy and himself as they walked up to the remains. He imagined Kathy turning away from the sight of it, crumpling to the ash-laden ground. She'll be inconsolable — stricken with grief, he figured.

Suddenly the return visit did not seem like such a good idea. Their dream home had become a nightmare and the nightmare was only beginning. New somber narratives had been written for each of the Scalari's lives and no amount of wishing, hoping and praying would change that. They would all have to live with the dark truth of it during every waking hour and even while they slept. *And where will we sleep?* That reality punched Frank in the gut. The house and every treasure inside of it was gone. He knew that much. All that remained would be the chimney and five-foot high cinder block foundation at the front. Whatever didn't burn would be at the bottom in a twisted, melted ash heap. The wood floor and everything above it — the bedrooms, the kitchen and the bathrooms — would have collapsed downward as it burned, falling into the five-foot high space under the house. The wood-burning stove from the family room would be down there in one piece, more or less. Frank visualized a thick blanket of gray ash covering their five acres. A burial shroud.

The branches stacked in the pile behind the house would have totally vaporized. Some of the tree trunks might still exist. A few blackened but not completely burned.

Frank snapped out of it when he read the familiar sign ahead to his right: HIGHWAY 79 OFF RAMP 1 1/2 MILES.

He moved over to the right lane and hit rewind on the coming catastrophe, steeling himself against its reality, 20 miles ahead. *We drive through the green gate. The metal barn is blown apart, none of the walls are standing, black rectangles where stalls used to be.*

Kathy had just one object on her mind, the fire inspection receipt. *It's my fault. I should've found it.* She repeated this over and over in her mind. The sleepless nights had caught up with her. She felt ruined. Early morning sunshine blazed through the ash-smeared windshield. She closed her eyes. She was in the house again, looking for the receipt, frantically pulling drawer after drawer out and dumping them on the floor. Kathy was on her knees on the kitchen floor tossing papers over one shoulder then the other. She looked up to her kitchen cabinets then scanned right, toward the sink. The junk drawer next to the sink. It stuck in her mind. She felt something thud in her heart. She had found it. There was the receipt, folded in thirds. She had placed the document there the day of the inspection so it wouldn't be lost in a pile of less important papers. In her anguish during the fire, she'd forgotten what she did with it. Tires thumped rhythm to the concrete below. Frank looked over at his wife. Kathy opened her eyes.

"I know where it is."

"What?" Frank asked.

"The insurance receipt. Or I know where it *was*. It doesn't matter now."

Frank stared out at the freeway without responding. He was uncertain about their options. If the insurance company was going to play hardball, there was only one recourse. They would have to file a lawsuit. Even if they won, it would cost thousands of dollars to sue a well-funded insurance company, and given the scope of this fire, they were probably standing in a long line when it came to insurance troubles. He grimaced. He didn't like the idea of going to court. He liked science. In a courtroom, you never knew how things would end up. It could go on for years. Where would they get the money for that? Where would they live? *How* would they live?

Frank took the off-ramp north under the freeway and onto Highway 79. It didn't look *too* bad close to the Interstate. Most of the pine and oak trees were not burned, but just north of the junction to Pine Valley the scene transformed into an apocalyptic mix of blackened rocks and ground and the sooted remains of almost every pine, oak or manzanita. Charcoaled trees full of scorched leaves or needles were everywhere. Smoke from thousands of hot spots filled the high valley as hundreds of firefighters in bright yellow and brown fire suits dotted the vast blackened landscape for miles. It was surreal.

A fire chief from the California Department of Forestry was conducting a checkpoint up ahead. Frank read the yellow sign along the right road shoulder:

ALL TRAFFIC MUST STOP! ACCESS TO THIS FIRE AREA IS RESTRICTED TO MOTORISTS WITH PHOTO I.D. AND PROOF OF RESIDENCE!

He pulled up to the end of the short line of vehicles and stopped. Kathy watched a ruddy captain in a white fireman's hat bend down to speak to a young man in a blue Corvette. The fireman straightened and extended his right arm. His index finger pointed the driver back in the direction he came from. Two minutes later Frank slowly pulled up.

"May I see your driver's license, sir?"

Frank handed it to the fireman. He focused on the picture, back to Frank, then down to the address. He knew where this was and hesitated before speaking.

"Uh, folks...Uhh...I...uh... know where you live. Below Poco Montana, right?"

"Yes, that's our place," said Kathy, leaning on Frank, hanging on every word.

"You're free to go. Be very careful as you drive, watch for downed power lines, some might still be live. And don't linger under the burned trees next to the road. Some of them have fallen already."

"You said you know where we live," Frank said. "What do you have to tell me?"

The fireman couldn't suppress his craggy frown. "I'm sorry, Frank. It's all gone."

Kathy let out a whispered gasp, covering it quickly with her hand. How many times would this surprise her? She turned to stare out the passenger side window so as not to share her emotion. Frank drove forward, whatever slim hope he had now vanished. He traveled slowly along, picking their way through the flaming obstacle course that Highway 79 had become. Red-hot tree branches on the highway had to be driven around as flames flared continuously here and there. Fire crews and their trucks were fanned out in assigned grid squares dousing hot spots across the scorched terrain on both sides of the road. Just past the south end of the lake, Kathy looked to see if The Edelweiss was still standing. The Tyrolean-styled restaurant with yellow, red and green chalet accent stripes around each feature had stood on the western side of the lake for decades. Blonde waitresses in stiff pigtails and frilly skirts were Kathy's memory of the place. She and Frank ate there years ago. The atmosphere had been so charming.

"Frank, look! It's gone! The Edelweiss is gone!"

Only the foundation remained. The restaurant had been reduced to a pile of ash-filled debris with a burned out commercial range and griddle still standing where the kitchen had been.

The surface of the shallow lake was black, the water full of ash and soot. The bait store and boat dock survived. The fire fighters had won a hard-fought victory for them. Previously secluded homes along the western side of the lake were secluded no longer. Nearly every tree burned to black, scorched leaves or needles still clinging. Nearly every house was now reduced to a desolate brick chimney. A stark lack of green dominated the view of macabre devastation.

Frank turned the SUV to the left, his familiar turn uphill onto Engineer's Road. The little volunteer fire station was undamaged, but as the couple drove toward the summit of North Peak, Frank and Kathy witnessed complete carnage.

"Oh my God! Look at this!" Kathy cried out. Tears traced down her cheeks at the terrible sight. It looked as if no tree, no house, no living creature on North Peak, northernmost of the three Cuyamaca Mountains escaped being destroyed. Near the summit lay a new horror.

"Oh no, the poor deer," cried Kathy.

The blackened remains of a mule deer doe and fawn lay not far off the road. The mother deer was tightly curled around the fawn in what appeared to be an attempt to shield her little one as the firestorm passed over them. The couple drove by dozens of destroyed homes within the smoldering charcoal forest, the cremated remains of the once beautiful woods now displaying their formerly hidden locations. The high, flat mountaintop had been stripped naked. New ocean views created in one night. As they crested over the western ridge, Kathy spotted something.

"Stop the car, Frank."

"Why?"

"Just stop the car for me, please, I see something."

Frank pulled over just off the road near the summit. As they exited the Suburban, the strong smell of fire overwhelmed them. It was inescapable. Powdered ash puffed up around their footsteps as they walked together to what used to be a picturesque overlook.

"Look at Middle Peak!" Frank cried. "*Look* at it!"

Middle Peak, to the south of them, with its cone-shaped crown and steep slope is the watershed for Ah-ha'-Mi-Ah-ha,' the stream at the bottom of it. Not one tree remained. The scene was heartbreaking. Flickers of orange fire and wisps of white smoke were spread throughout the vast expanse of what had been a lush pine covered mountain, now reduced to a colossal cinder.

Kathy was not looking at Middle Peak. She was staring northwest from the overlook and far down the mountain. What she saw just wasn't possible. Perhaps the exhaustion had taken control of her and she was hallucinating. Yet, she stared and stared and there it was somehow.

Green.

In the middle of the vast, charred forest, an impossible patch of green was visible. Verdant and vibrant against the surrounding blackness, it appeared scrubbed fresh, a beacon of clean and vivid springtime. It was surrounded by the charred remains of the merciless firestorm.

"Frank, do you see it?"

"I see it. I don't believe it, but I see it."

They were both thinking the same thing. Their eyes had deceived them. A quick blast of wind threw ash into their faces from below the ridge. They quickly retreated to the Suburban. Frank slowly pulled back onto the road and drove past the little turnout where last Tuesday his neighbors helped them to finally get Neo into the trailer. As he negotiated the switchbacks, he remembered how beautiful their mountain had been just four days ago. The Scalari's dreams and the dreams of so many others had been destroyed in a couple of hours last Tuesday evening.

Kathy saw a familiar blue pickup truck down a long, burned out driveway. "There's the man who helped you with the ramp!"

She watched him as they passed by, bent over, wearing a dust mask, sifting through the ashes of his destroyed home. This sad scene was repeated all the way down the mountain. The gravity of all the Scalari's neighbors now homeless overwhelmed Kathy. She sobbed quietly, unable to suppress her grief. Frank's eyes filled with tears, too, powerless to make it better, to remove any of Kathy's pain. He eased the Suburban around the last switchback, headed north and spotted the familiar old concrete retaining wall that marked the straightaway for home. They were close now. Frank's throat began to constrict. His tongue stuck to the roof of his mouth.

"There's Tom Wilby!" Kathy pointed. "Oh no! His house! The barn!"

Tom was standing in the ash-filled concrete foundation of what remained of his home. He was holding a burned piece of metal in his hands, salvaged from the ashes. Tom had to laugh as he held it out from his body and read the cheerful yellow reminder to: 'KEEP YOUR TIPS UP!' He was still smiling and he waved as the Scalaris drove by. "They must think I've gone nuts," he said to himself. This brief mental respite from his misery soon dissipated. Tom placed the seared metal sign in a trash bag, picked up a flat shovel, and resumed sifting through two feet of grimy ashes in what had been the living room.

UNCOVERED

State Hwy 79

Lake Cuyamaca

State Hwy 79

Frank & Kathy's road home

A patch of green

The neighbors sifting ashes

JAMUL 9:10 A.M.

I removed the fiberglass top to the pool filter for the fourth time that Saturday morning. *Black again.* I had brushed and scooped and back flushed, but the pool water remained dark. It was the same story for everyone in the county to one degree or another. The Cedar Fire had left its final curse: grimy, sooty ash. Joni had taken the hose and gone to work on a stubborn layer of black on the concrete patio in front of the house. Neither one of us were having any luck. But that wasn't what was on our minds. Our problems were trivial. All we could think about was the Scalari's.

I brought the filthy pool filter from the backyard to Joni and the hose. "The ash chokes the filter every ten minutes," I complained. "Do you think they know yet?"

"They've got to be very close, if they're not home already," said Joni.

She had prayed for years for the Scalari family to receive the Lord. It hadn't happened. The previous Monday afternoon she had changed course. *Maybe a physical miracle is what it takes for them to accept the reality of you, Lord,* Joni had wondered.

That day she asked in Jesus' name for a supernatural wonder that only a sovereign God with absolute power could accomplish. The Lord had never failed to answer Joni's prayers, even when his answer was no. She would accept God's answer today too, whatever it was.

ENGINEERS ROAD 9:12 A.M.

The Scalari's heartbreak was nearly complete. Just a few hundred yards ahead sat the conclusion of their catastrophic week. The tires slowly rolled, the tears slowly flowed, and their stomachs quickly tightened. *Expect the worst and you're never disappointed,* thought Kathy.

Frank had planned ahead. He had bought two large sifters and two flat-edged shovels on Friday afternoon at the big home improvement store in Lemon Grove. Kathy had thrown in boxes of small and large clear plastic bags to sort and store whatever it was they were about to find. They would sift the ashes for hours like all their neighbors were doing, then they would drive back to her mom's place to decide what to do next. They would be welcome there for a long while, but neither of them wanted that. If Kathy had found the fire insurance receipt the insurance company would have set them up in a rental house. But she hadn't found it. It had gone up in smoke with the rest of her belongings.

A foreboding anticipation filled Kathy's heart. She turned her eyes to Frank. She saw the anguish on his face. He was powerless to hide it. Her rock was crumbling right in front of her and all she could do was watch...

Maybe Joni was right. Hell does exist. We're living though it.

One hundred yards away, now. Less than a football field. Frank glanced over at his quivering wife. Tears flooded down her cheeks. Their hearts raced. They felt like two doomed airline passengers after the wings have fallen off the jet. There was nothing left for them to do now but brace themselves.

Frank drove slowly forward. Kathy closed her eyes.

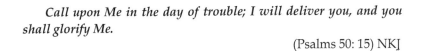

Call upon Me in the day of trouble; I will deliver you, and you shall glorify Me.

(Psalms 50: 15) NKJ

II

GOD AND FIRE

Chapter Eight
Treasure Field

"The kingdom of heaven is like treasure hidden in a field. When a man found it, he hid it again, and then in his joy went and sold all he had and bought that field."

(Matthew 13:44)

Chapter Eight
Treasure Field

He makes the winds his messengers, flames of fire his servants.
(Psalms 104:4)

9:15 A.M.

FRANK PULLED UP to the green metal gate and stopped. His jaw went slack.

He and Kathy both sat inside the SUV motionless.

The apple orchard was shining in the morning sun. The barn still stood. Its big breezeway doors were wide open.

"Open the gate, Frank," Kathy said finally.

Frank pushed the remote button. "It won't open. No power." He stepped out and choked in the ash-filled air. He pushed a hidden lever and manually opened the gate. Frank drove through the gate and turned right onto his property. The field to the south of them had burned to black right up to the property line. Then the black stopped. Frank stepped on the brake and eyed the vast smoldering acreage to his right.

Kathy was perplexed. "Why did it stop? It shouldn't have stopped, should it?"

Frank was incredulous. "I don't know. How could it?"

He spotted the weather-beaten chicken coop with its straw and chicken manure. It was undamaged. Small flames had burned the ground near the coop, but incredibly, had gone out somehow right in the middle of the dry grass.

Kathy sat pondering as Frank rolled the Suburban beside the barn's open breezeway. Inside of the barn sat a thick layer of pale straw. Several huge blackened oak trees were framed through the big doorway, looming large a few feet away on the easement road. She closed her eyes. *This is just not possible.* She opened them and stared at the floor of the car...at her new black work boots. She looked out her side window. *This can't be real. I'm dreaming again.* North of the barn the apple trees stood in neat rows with vivid green leaves and rose-and-green-colored apples hanging heavy on the branches.

"Kath. Do you see what I'm seeing?"

"I can't believe it. How? Frank, *how?*"

"I don't know. Our house. It's our *house*, Kath."

To the east, the house which Frank imagined to be destroyed, fallen into itself inside the cinder block foundation, still sat on its little hill. He parked between the barn and the house and they stepped out of the Suburban. They moved slowly and quietly, as if they did not want to disturb the what was before them. The big oak tree glittered in the sun, not a leaf even withered from the heat. The long swing rocked lazily in the chilly morning air. Kathy took a deep breath. She exhaled. She took another. That's when it hit her. Something was missing.

"Frank. Take a deep breath."

He sucked in as much air as he could hold. "Okay. Now what?"

"What do you smell?"

"Nothing." The word bounced around in his head *Nothing?* "Wait a minute. I don't smell any smoke."

Something else was missing. Frank looked down at a broad yellow carpet of foxtails between the barn and the house. Nothing. He scanned the orchard. *More nothing.*

"Kathy? Where is the ash?"

Kathy spun around slowly, eyeing every area of her property.

"There *is* no ash."

Frank slumped down onto the swing. The house loomed above him. It remained exactly as they had left it four days ago. Not a scorch-mark, not even any blistered paint. In fact, it had never looked better. It twinkled as if it had been pressure washed an hour ago—like the entire property had remained within the eye of a fiery hurricane throughout the firestorm—a calm, cool, five acre oasis.

Frank thought it through.

It should be like all the other houses we saw. We should be sifting an ash heap. What's going on?

Kathy led him up the dirt driveway. She stopped suddenly.

"Look at this!" she said, pointing at an oak tree just outside the fence. The trunk and branches were black all the way up to the top of the tree. Scorched leaves still clung to it. Kathy gawked at one particular limb that was still pointing its bony fingers at the south side of their house. The intruding branch had not burned.

"Do you see this?"

Frank was a little spooked. "I see it. I don't believe it but I see it."

The live oak's limb was black with thick soot like the rest of the tree until the limb passed over into the Scalari's airspace. There it returned to a healthy mottled gray. The leaves, ten feet over their heads, were a vibrant green. Kathy followed the healthy limb from near the side of her house to it's encompassing ring of black soot above the fence. She stared at Frank, eyes pleading, head cocked, waiting for an explanation.

"Frank. How is that possible?"

"Don't look at me, I have no idea."

They stared and stared. They were short of breath. Their hearts pounded. Frank turned his attention to the dumpster ten feet to the east. "Where did the covers go?" The rubber covers were gone. He peered down into the depths of the big metal box. Nothing at all remained inside. He noticed a change in it though. He bent down outside the box and saw that the hard rubber wheels of the dumpster were missing. The fire's heat had melted the wheels down to the metal rims.

Meanwhile, Kathy was standing a few feet away in a layer of ash that used to be the western end of the piled trunks. She was standing where four foot long, 20-inch-diameter pine tree trunks had been tightly stacked higher than her head four days ago. They were gone. All of them. Not a charcoal sized lump remained. It was as if the massive 12-cord powder keg of fuel never existed. Or somehow was lifted up and out of the physical world without damaging objects right next to it. The ash stood in a tidy four-inch-high, 50-foot-long rectangle entirely outside the Scalari property. From Kathy's position she was a scant twelve feet from the rear wooden porch and the back door of her home. Twelve feet. She was standing within an area which had generated temperatures near 2,000°F degrees last Tuesday night. That her house had not burned down was simply an impossibility, but what she saw on that wooden porch, which itself should not have existed, sent shivers throughout her entire body.

"Frank, *look!*" she said, pointing a trembling finger at the porch.

Frank's eyes widened. "How in the..." They walked to the porch and stood over a miracle.

Plastic bags.

Eight black plastic bags so thin a hair dryer could have melted a hole through them sat filled with clothes, photos and keepsakes, right where Kathy and Frank left them. Untouched. Pristine. No ash. No smell of smoke. Ash and soot were everywhere outside of their property. Inches of it. The smell of fire was overpowering, yet inside the boundary the air was sweet. Nowhere else in Cuyamaca Woods was such a dense collection of fuel gathered, yet barns and homes ignited as the heat from the firestorm came near them — the straw in the barns and paper in the houses spontaneously combusted as the outside temperature became the inside temperature. *BOOM!* They were gone. What in the natural world could shield a home, a tree or a plastic bag full of pictures from searing heat hot enough to melt metal? Frank knew the answer to that question. Nothing. In the *natural* world. To stand 150 feet from the temperatures generated within the raging pine tree trunks would cause extreme discomfort. To stand within 100 feet would cause flash burns to unprotected skin. Twelve feet? Spontaneous combustion for most any substance. Metal softens, hard rubber wheels burn off, clothes, hair, even *skin* bursts into flames. Death. Yet here the plastic bags sat.

Something else had been at the back of Kathy's mind. She noticed it in her peripheral vision earlier but shelved it among closer wonders. She gently placed her hand on Frank's shoulder as he rummaged through one of the plastic bags and tapped for his attention. He straightened up. They looked at each other, neither of them saying a word. Kathy led him with her eyes toward objects of new interest at the eastern boundary, 50 feet away.

Kindling.

Frank let out a gasp. This was the wood pile he had feared the most before they left with the horses last Tuesday. He remembered feeling hopeless as he sprinkled this 100-foot-long tinderbox with a hose, yet here it was. *This has to be a mistake. My eyes are playing tricks on me.*

The couple made their way uphill to the long jumbled pile.

"How could these not have burned?" Frank shook his head. He knew full well it wasn't possible. "These branches had to burn! They *had* to!" He lifted a few small twigs off the top as if to verify the reality of them, then he focused past the dirt road and onto the empty space where the log stack stood four days ago. He closed his eyes and visualized all that wood on fire. He could feel the torrid heat. He could see the titanic flames, the terrible destruction, the constant shower of embers flying in every direction, and the sound of the furious wind flowing into the pile of burning trunks. He opened his eyes. The logs were gone, just ash remained. Frank began to shake. "I am a *physicist*. I am a *scientist*. There is a scientific solution for any phenomenon!" He dropped the dry twigs back onto the pile. An unaccustomed emotion overtook him. His eyes filled because of it.

Kathy was standing on the dirt driveway, squared up with the eastern boundary and looking down the long pile of small and large pine branches. It was quite easy to see where her property ended now. A sharp black line hundreds of feet long was before her, stretching out parallel to the branches and true to the property line. In some spots the branches were stacked just an inch or two away from the blackened ground beyond them. The flames burned up dry pine needles, sawdust and twigs on the ground beyond the arbitrary and invisible boundary, but not on the Scalari's side of it. A thick layer of rust-colored pine needles was divided sharply — burned and unburned.

Kathy felt goose bumps. "I've got to call Joni!"

Frank moved four of the plastic bags out of the center of the rear landing and held the back door open for her.

"*Brrrr!* It's freezing in here!" Kathy said as she descended the open staircase to the family room.

Frank flipped a light switch: "The batteries are dead."

Kathy picked up the phone hoping for a dial tone. "The phone's dead too."

"The land line must've burned up," Frank concluded. "You could try the *spot.*"

There was a 10' x 10' area inside the apple orchard that usually allowed her cell phone work. Kathy stepped out the door onto the front balcony and jumped down the stairs to share the good news with her friend. She hurried into the orchard, brushing through apple-filled branches. The aroma was an intoxicating mix of spring rain and tree-ripened fruit. The apple orchard had not only survived, it had flourished. Every fruit tree was clean. Kathy positioned herself and looked down at her cell phone.

Two bars. Better than before the fire, she thought as she dialed our number.

Against incredibly long odds, I, *not* Joni, answered the phone. I listened in astonishment as Kathy related what she was seeing in a reverent whisper. "*Greg. Nothing burned! It's all here! There's no ash! There's no smell of smoke! There's no smell of fire! It's like a religious experience!*"

A feeling of reverence, awe, love and conviction filled me as I instantly realized that God had answered Joni and Danielle's prayers. Conviction because I hadn't put my faith in God on the line like my wife and daughter had done. During the fire, I remembered thinking:

God, this is a really bad fire. Their house and property are going to burn. I don't want to pray for something so impossible, so nakedly supernatural, then feel lost when all that's left is a soot-covered chimney.

I had never heard Kathy acknowledge the possibility of God until right then.

"That's *God,* Kathy. You're on holy ground. He is awesome! He is so *awesome!* We're so happy for you! Here's Joni."

Joni, standing beside me, was in joyful tears, trembling over God's answer.

"That's exactly what I prayed for, Kathy! That's what I've been telling you! He's real! Danielle prayed too. She asked Him to protect your house, your barn, and your orchard."

I watched as Joni held the phone to her ear, listening, and I saw her expression change. She began shaking her head. "What? No. No, it *isn't* that God let all the other homes burn...But Kathy, it isn't *about* fair. It's *not.* It's about grace. You received something you didn't deserve. God's grace."

It sounded to me like it was going to take more than a physical miracle to see Kathy raise a white flag over such deep spiritual entrenchments. Our eyes met as Joni listened. She looked broken hearted. She shook her head.

"But... But... It's a fallen world, Kathy."

As I listened to Joni's side of the conversation I became aware of just how hard it is to joyfully receive miraculously good news from God. For me, it came with a large measure of guilt. I had not been up to the task. My faith was too weak. I had adopted a defensive posture. For Kathy and Frank, it brought confusion. Their confidence in what they believed to be fact and what they believed to be fiction had been broken. For Joni and Danielle, however, this was what happened when you prayed in faith believing. God answered those prayers.

After a few minutes the cell connection was lost.

"I will have mercy on whom I will have mercy, and I will have compassion on whom I will have compassion."

(Exodus 33:19)

TREASURE FIELD

SMALL WONDER

"Are not two sparrows sold for a penny? Yet not one of them will fall to the ground apart from the will of your Father. And even the very hairs of your head are all numbered."

(Matthew 10: 29-30)

After the cell connection dropped, Kathy walked through the southern end of the apple orchard. Something familiar caught her eye. The strong Santa Ana wind that began to blow last Saturday morning slammed this object against and partially through the old wire fence a little northwest of the barn. The insignificant item straddling her western property line was not on anyone's radar screen so far as she knew. Kathy stood in front of the thing, a white-as-snow and black-as-charcoal mystery. She studied it carefully. It was hung up in the fence a foot off the ground. Kathy bent down to within inches of it, stunned by the details of the wooden marvel. Frank came to her as she reached out to touch the small wonder, positioned 35 feet northwest of the barn.

As it happened, this four-foot-long object *had* in fact been on someone's radar screen. "Do you see what I'm seeing? Look at this," said Kathy. Frank came alongside.

"Can anyone hide in secret places so that I cannot see him?" declares the LORD. "Do not I fill heaven and earth?" declares the LORD.

(Jeremiah 23:24)

The wooden stool.

A common white bar stool before the fire, this miraculous artifact had blown against and partially through the old wire fence last Saturday. It was burned and unburned. Started and stopped. Half of the seat was now charcoal along with a small part of the legs beneath it, the flames having stopped on a sharp diagonal in obedience to the property line. Kathy touched the stool, her fingers tracing over the smooth white side of the seat, then over the rough charcoaled side. Frank squatted to take a closer look. The seat of the thing looked like a giant black-white cookie.

"Frank?"

He shrugged. "Oh, Kath. I dunno."

Outside each of the Scalari's property lines flames continuously flared up from hot spots on the ground or inside of smoldering trees. In the late afternoon Frank and Kathy tried their best to put out a flaming oak tree that was burning outside of their property and not too far from the pile of kindling behind the house. Fiery embers shot up and out of the red-hot ruptured trunk of the old oak, and Frank was terrified that what had been the surest combustible collection of fuel before the fire remained so now. They threw shovels full of dirt into the flaring trunk but the fire kept restarting.

"Let's take a break," Frank said.

The couple walked down the sooty hill outside of their eastern property line and stopped beside the long pile of branches. Both of them leaned on their new shovels. They were tired, emotionally drained and physically spent. Kathy took a long look at the jumbled kindling stretching on in both directions beyond her, then at her soot-covered boots. She focused on the blackened ground beneath them and became more than a little frustrated at her husband's lack of a satisfactory explanation.

"*You're* the expert. Tell me what's going on here. C'mon, Mr. Physicist! I want to hear your scientific theory for what I'm looking at."

She glared at him, her arms cramping from frantic shoveling. Frank looked down at the sharp black line where the fire resumed destruction a few inches outside of the piled branches. He thought about it for a good long time, quickly formulating a list of potential explanations, then discarding them one by one until he settled upon his strongest option.

"Wind currents?"

"Wind currents? *Wind currents?* That's all you've got?"

"Yeah, that's all I've got. Pretty weak isn't it?"

Kathy began to grin. "*Wind currents...*" she muttered.

Frank laughed. Kathy watched her husband's face in the soft fading light, the flaming tree unfocused behind him. *CRACK!* The flames inside the tree exploded — doubling in size. The oak began to tilt. Frank watched the flaming, collapsing tree reflected in his wife's terrified eyes. *CRASH!* The big tree collapsed with a loud thump, shaking the ground under their feet. The heavy trunk fell directly onto the spot where the couple had been standing two minutes before. Kathy's knees began to buckle. Frank caught her before she fell.

"We would've been killed! No more! Let the firemen do it!" said Kathy.

Frank, still speechless, was gaping at twenty-foot flames coming from the midst of the crumpled oak; flames that he and his wife would have been trapped under, burning alive with no one around to save them. He took his trembling wife in his arms in a tight embrace. He kissed her again and again all over her face.

"Okay. No more fire fighting. I promise. Go on in the house, it's getting dark. I'll start the generator."

Frank watched his shaken wife disappear through the back door. He stood there in the lavender light, backlit by the crackling bonfire of a tree forty feet to the east. It was a timeless moment. Weightless even. Like levitating inside his own body. It was a feeling that only comes when a man is quite certain he has just cheated death. He took a deep breath. He exhaled. In a single day, Frank had been confounded by the miraculous and confronted with his own mortality. He had unknowingly tap-danced on the edge of a great unknown chasm and had suddenly lost his balance. What could he hold onto? How could he explain the unexplainable? His life had been forever diverted—hijacked by what appeared for all the world to be a supernatural phenomenon. But Frank didn't *believe* in the supernatural. It made his head hurt. He needed help—guidance from somebody, but who? He gazed up to the darkening sky and he remembered.

Frank smiled. "Old Jenks."

He recalled his grad school cosmology class and the high-pitched, nasal drone of Professor Jenkins. Frank pictured himself in his seat, 4th from the bottom, 5th from the aisle. He remembered how he used to stare at the back of the professor's balding head as he scribbled an equation on his slate gray chalkboard. Jenkins would turn around, his icy blue eyes piercing the crowd, waiting until he had captured every student's attention...

"Ladies and gentlemen. The universe is clearly expanding, but there's a problem. It isn't happening fast enough. When we add up the combined mass of the cosmos there simply isn't enough stuff to hold it all together like this. What is keeping the universe from flying apart? It *is* a mystery." Professor Jenkins jabbed his stick of chalk at the insolvable point of his equation. "So what could be holding it all together? Some invisible force? Is some sort of dark energy braking the expansion of the entire universe? What could this powerful invisible force be? *Hmmmmm?* Maybe miniature black holes are the answer. Or, perhaps one of you has a different theory. Does anyone here have a quarrel with the late, great, Mr. Darwin? Would one of you dare to admit your belief in the supernatural? Can anyone name for me an otherwise brilliant physicist who believed in a directing intelligent creator? In Santa Claus in the *sky?*"

Nervous glances filled the room.

"I don't see any hands. Come now class. Surely *one* of you burgeoning physicists knows the answer to my harmless little question? *No?* All right then my pointy-headed cowards...Einstein. Albert Einstein believed in God," declared Jenkins. "He believed God created the universe and then walked away."

The roomful of postgraduate students let out a collective gasp. Professor Jenkins howled with laughter, waving his arms at the floor, demanding quiet. Then came a breathless silence.

"He was also famously of the opinion that: 'God does not play dice.' I'm not so sure about that. If God *does* play dice, what sort of dice does God play?"

Frank began to grin. He raised his hand.

"Mr. Scalari?"

"Loaded dice, sir?"

Professor Jenkins nodded his head. "Clever boy, such a clever boy..."

Frank's reveries faded. Professor Jenkins was dead, after all. But what would *he* have made of all of this? Would he have had the answers? *No, the old man wouldn't have understood it anymore than I do.*

Frank walked past the photovoltaic panels and up to the door of the pump house. He opened it and stepped inside. Reaching up to the high shelf, he found his big flashlight and switched it on. He trained the fat yellow beam on the cap of the generator's fuel tank. He unscrewed it and aimed his light down into the deep pool of diesel oil.

"Half a tank."

Half a tank will run the generator about 8 hours. He made a mental note to buy some more fuel. He pushed the green button above the red kill switch and the generator came to life.

Frank walked downhill toward the front of the warmly lit house. A cold breeze kicked up in the blackening twilight. The remnants of the firestorm glowed cherry-red behind him as he climbed the stairs. Before climbing the last step, he paused in the darkness to peek at Kathy as she washed at the sink. Frank watched her for long stolen moments, reliving vivid and pleasant memories of her, the years seeming to fall away. She deserved an answer about all this. He'd always been able to provide one. Until now.

The aroma of freshly brewed French-roast coffee filled the kitchen. Kathy poured two tall steaming cups. She heard the balcony door. "I made us some coffee."

"Strong, I hope. You'll freak out when you see all the hot spots out there," said Frank as he walked into the kitchen. He wrapped his arms around his wife's waist as she added creamer to their cups. He rested his chin on her shoulder as she stirred.

Kathy couldn't let it go. She sent up a flare.

"Joni said today that she and Danielle prayed for this to happen. They prayed for a big miracle so we'd know that God is real. She told me Danielle prayed for the barn, and the house and the apple orchard. She even prayed for the big oak with the kid's swing. But I told her that I've just always been lucky. Things *always* go my way. Even when I was a girl I was very lucky. What do you think?"

Frank paused to consider his answer, careful not to include wind currents. "Whatever it was, it wasn't because of some prayer. I tried that when I was twelve. My Uncle Leo?"

"When you were still in Catholic school?"

"Yeah. I loved Leo. He loved me too. The last time I saw him was in the hospital. He'd had another heart attack. He looked bad. So I pulled my box of religious trinkets out from under my bed and I prayed. Imagine that. I balled my eyes out. It was the only time I prayed the rosary for anybody. But Uncle Leo died. I figured, what's the point? There's no power in prayer 'cause ain't *no*-body listening. So I became I scientist. Now this. Cruel, isn't it? There *is* an explanation, I just haven't figured it out yet. But I will. I promise you. Then we're gonna' have to break it to those Jesus freak friends of ours. You know, Kath, not every house on this mountain burned."

"But, it wasn't just our house, Frank. Our *weeds* didn't burn. Our *trees* didn't burn. No embers flew in. Explain that," she challenged. "What's your theory? How did this house survive?"

Frank dug deep, trying to remember everything he had seen or read about the Cedar Fire during the days spent at her mom's place. Then he recalled a conversation he and Kathy had in September with Tom and Sharon Wilby. They had stopped by to introduce themselves and to gather information about the newcomers for the rest of the mountain.

"Do you remember when Tom and Sharon came by not long after we moved in?" Kathy nodded. "Sharon told you about our house being built within the sacred hunting grounds of the Indians a hundred and fifty years ago. Maybe that had something to do with it. Why would God spare *us* while everyone else around us came back to nothing?"

Good question. He has a point—this was Indian country. So Kathy, being somewhat satisfied, dropped the subject.

LAVA   6:30 P.M.

Every ember, every flicker of flame was visible for miles around as Kathy and Frank sat outside on the balcony drinking coffee, both of them bundled warmly against the cold early evening air. Poco Montana's eastern slope glowed bright red above them, lava seemingly filling dozens of tiny craters. Frank set his cup on the cafe' table between them, following the warm vapor from it until it disappeared a few inches above the rim. Kathy set her cup down near his and noticed something strangely absent.

"No red spots. We don't have any."

Hundreds of hot spots glowed all around their valley, revealing the firestorm's ferocious paths. Each fully consumed tree had burned down to a glowing root ball and each of them was slowly roasting underground. Kathy could clearly see even small details everywhere else in her vision but *her* property was dark. It was as if they were the only residents who didn't put up any Christmas lights. Their neighbors had bought out the store.

Frank rose to his feet. Below Poco Montana's eastern summit, the top half of a 120-foot-high time bomb of a sugar pine exploded in flames. Frank watched in horror as an orb of brilliant fire billowed up to the black sky and broke apart, cascading down in small flaming pieces to the scorched earth below. Then came the sound of the explosion. His jaw muscles clenched.

"We've got to find some firefighters in the morning. I doubt any of them believe there's a house left in this valley to protect."

Kathy took a long draw from her cup. The warm aroma filled her nostrils. In front of her, halfway to the summit, the largest of the hot spots erupted, belching hot black smoke like a small volcano.

"Frank. I was sure we'd lost everything. Our photographs of the kids. The house. The barn. Everything we owned. We were ruined."

"What about the insurance company," added Frank. "We were going to lose, you know."

"I know it," said Kathy. "Where would we have gotten the money to fight back? Where would we have lived? But, this is creepy. Can't you feel it?"

"I feel it. Look around us. This place is right out of an old Twilight Zone episode. The one where the guy flips a coin and it stands up on end? All day long he can hear people's thoughts. Until the coin falls. I keep thinking I'm going to look back at the house and it'll be an ash heap—the way it should've been. Or in flames. Or we'll go to sleep tonight in our bed and wake up on fire!"

Kathy's jaw dropped. "So much for sleeping in our bed. Better make a fresh pot..."

The Scalaris were inhabiting a mystery beyond anything they had ever encountered. Either something supremely supernatural had occurred or something with no explanation whatsoever. They were learning a very old lesson about a miraculous manifestation of God's power. For believers *and* nonbelievers...

There will be fear. There will be trembling.

If God had miraculously spared their property, Kathy and Frank had nothing to worry about—no fire on earth can defy Him. Elijah, the Old Testament prophet, knew a thing or two about God and fire. He could've told them. He had a showdown on Mount Carmel with 450 prophets of a false god named Baal...

ELIJAH

"Then you call on the name of your god, and I will call on the name of the Lord. The god who answers by fire—he is God."

Then all the people said, "What you say is good."

Elijah said to the prophets of Baal, "Choose one of the bulls and prepare it first, since there are so many of you. Call on the name of your god, but do not light the fire." So they took the bull given them and prepared it.

Then they called on the name of Baal from morning till noon. "Baal, answer us!" they shouted. But there was no response; no one answered. And they danced around the altar they had made.

At noon Elijah began to taunt them. "Shout louder!" he said. "Surely he is a god! Perhaps he is deep in thought, or busy, or traveling. Maybe he is sleeping and must be awakened." So they shouted louder and slashed themselves with swords and spears, as was their custom, until their blood flowed. Midday passed, and they continued their frantic prophesying until the time for the evening sacrifice. But there was no response, no one answered, no one paid attention.

Then Elijah said to all the people, "Come here to me." They came to him, and he repaired the altar of the LORD, which had been torn down. Elijah took twelve stones, one for each of the tribes descended from Jacob, to whom the word of the LORD had come, saying, "Your name shall be Israel." With the stones he built an altar in the name of the LORD, and he dug a trench around it large enough to hold two seahs of seed. He arranged the wood, cut the bull into pieces and laid it on the wood. Then he said to them, "Fill four large jars with water and pour it on the offering and on the wood."

"Do it again," he said, and they did it again.

"Do it a third time," he ordered, and they did it the third time. The water ran down around the altar and even filled the trench.

At the time of the sacrifice, the prophet Elijah stepped forward and prayed: "LORD, the God of Abraham, Isaac and Israel, let it be known today that you are God in Israel and that I am your servant and have done all these things at your command. Answer me, LORD, answer me, so these people will know that you, LORD, are God, and that you are turning their hearts back again."

Then the fire of the LORD fell and burned up the sacrifice, the wood, the stones and the soil, and also licked up the water in the trench.

When all the people saw this, they fell prostrate and cried, "The LORD – he is God! The LORD – he is God!

(1Kings 18:24-39)

TREASURE FIELD

The pile of branches behind the house wouldn't burn. They're inches *inside* the eastern property line.

A pile of logs, 8 feet high & 50 feet long, were vaporized in the fire, inches *outside* the southern property line.

Chapter Nine
Hidden Treasure

*The genuine realist, if he is an unbeliever, will always find
strength and ability to disbelieve in the miraculous, and if he is
confronted with a miracle as an irrefutable fact he would rather
disbelieve his own senses than admit the fact. Faith does not spring
from the miracle, but the miracle from faith.*

FYODOR DOSTOEVKY

Chapter Nine
Hidden Treasure

SUNDAY, NOVEMBER 2, 2003

7:10 A.M.

FRANK AND KATHY had gone to bed around eleven. The couple's quite rational fear of the Cedar Fire's remnants had finally been overcome by an overwhelming fatigue. The muffled sound of a Jake-brake quietly intruded into their bedroom as they slept.

A white fire truck with a Texas shaped decal on its door descended the steep grade down Engineers Road. The crew's captain sat in the front passenger seat. He craned around and looked out the rear window of the crew cab and he laughed. Two of his firemen were standing on the rear platform of the long pumper truck grasping handholds. The younger one, who looked to be about nineteen, was dancing. He whooped and hollered around every turn.

GUG-GUG-GUG-GUG

Frank and Kathy were startled awake by the sound. The fire truck had pulled up to the green gate by the time they came downstairs. The purr of the big diesel filled the valley.

Frank squinted. "We've got a pumper truck out front near the gate. It's white. Must be from another state."

Four firefighting Texans fell out of both sides of the cab and two more hopped off the rear. The fastest of them, the boyish blond from the rear deck, was already in the orchard.

"Y'all, come here! Look-it this!"

By the time Kathy and Frank walked out, the hungry Texans were filling their bellies with Julian apples.

"Sorry folks, we didn't see you up there," said the crew's captain. He was older than the others by more than a decade.

"Help yourselves. Eat all you want. I'm Frank. This is my wife Kathy. We're just happy that you know we're here."

The captain was surveying the property. "We heard a rumor about this place from some firemen from L.A. County. They were here a day after the fire came through. My boys wanted to see if what we heard was true."

The captain watched one of his firemen, a 5' 10" powerfully built African American man as he scanned the acreage. The fireman turned around slowly, smiling incredulously and shaking his head as he took in the surrounding lack of devastation.

"You satisfied now, son?" asked the fire chief.

"Captain. Somebody sure knows how to pray."

"Don't jump to any conclusions. Remember your training," said the captain.

After a few minutes the firemen got down to business. The captain fanned his men out in different directions, positioning them around the most active flare-ups. Their job now was to dig and douse hot spots. They spread out into the surrounding valley and hillside, each of them with a shovel, an ax and a pressure tank of water strapped to their backs to begin the dull task of waiting. Waiting until the last buried fire pit smothered or burned out.

The captain took the baby-faced 19-year-old fireman with him as they followed Frank behind the house to investigate a rising plume of smoke. The captain trudged uphill to the burning oak tree. Flames continued to flare from the ruptured trunk. Frank and the young man stopped on the sooted ground outside the stacked branches.

"We tried to put it out yesterday but the flames kept coming back," Frank explained. "It collapsed right after we walked away."

"When oaks are burning down inside the trunk you can't put

'em out unless you bulldoze 'em out of the ground,"said the captain. "You and your wife are lucky."

Frank watched the 19-year-old as he gawked at the collection of kindling. "Did y'all just stack up all this wood yesterday?" asked the Texan.

Frank got nose to nose with him. *This ought'a be fun to watch.* Five-seconds passed without a word between them. The firefighter broke eye contact, stared down at his boots, at the blackened ground, then back into Frank's eyes.

"Well, *did* 'ya?"

Frank smiled. "Nope. All this wood is exactly where it was before the fire." He watched the young man's eyes widen.

"Sir! That's impossible!" He looked at the woodpile. "No way! Captain? Did you hear that? How could that be true? No way! *No way!*"

The captain wasn't amused. "Calm down and go to work on this flamer in front of me. Open it up."

The fire pup jogged up to his captain's position and began digging eagerly around the base of the trunk. Embers were flying. The captain walked down to Frank, who was still standing next to the wood. "He's a good firefighter but he's, *mmmm,* you might say he's high-strung."

Frank smiled. "I had the same reaction when I saw all this wood still sitting here yesterday."

"What did you do with the trunks?" asked the captain.

Frank motioned with his hand. He walked the five steps between the end of the branches and the middle of where the trunks used to be and stopped smack in the midst of ashes settling around his shoes. He turned to face the fire chief. "This is where they were."

The hair stood up on the back of the captain's neck. All his experience with fire characteristics began screaming at him. He knew. Right then he knew. This house should not exist.

"What were the dimensions of the pile of trunks?" he asked.

"About eight feet high and about fifty feet long. They were cut in four-foot sections," Frank answered.

The captain began calculating as he walked into the ash and up to a protruding stump. "This one of your cut down pines?"

"Yes, and the one a little farther down the fence," said Frank.

"I figure you had ten to twelve cords of logs sitting here. Is that what you had?"

Frank pursed his lips. "Twelve."

The captain ambled up to the dumpster and peered into its clean insides. "What did you have in here, Frank?"

Frank hesitated to tell him. "*Uhhh*...well, we were in a panic that last day and I...uh, I dumped all my fuel cans in there. I didn't know what else to do with them."

"Did this thing have plastic covers?"

Frank chuckled. "Yes, it had rubber wheels, too. I closed it before we left."

The fire chief bent at the waist and ogled the steel rims of the dumpster's wheels minus the rubber. He straightened, his left hand clutching the rim of the dumpster, then turned his gaze to the wooden porch at the back door of the house a few feet away. A perplexed expression formed on his face, eyebrows stretching skyward. He began to shake his head slowly.

"No way. Nope."

He was uncomfortable with what the physical evidence was telling him. Less than a week ago, something prevented this house and property from being consumed. Whatever that something was, it had to be more powerful than the firestorm itself.

Water had been of little use against the Cedar Fire. Structure protection was possible with enough men and equipment. A skillful back-burn helped save the old gold mining town of Julian last Tuesday and he and his crew had been a part of it. Two walls of fire, one tall, the other small, had crashed into each other like two converging wakes on water, canceling the momentum of both. They simply snuffed each other out. The Texans had passed through this area on Engineers Road that afternoon in a long procession of fire pumpers en-route to Julian. The captain recalled their trip down from Lake Cuyamaca: *A parked line of cars headed the other way... the drivers were gathered outside behind a horse trailer... Strange. They were clapping for joy.*

Frank watched the captain walk between the dumpster and the house, stopping midway between them both.

"What do you think, Captain?"

The captain was pushing away a word in his mind, suppressing it with all his mental might, but it was like trying to ignore a beautiful woman as she passed on the street. His very spirit cried out inside him.

The word was *miracle*.

Frank stood there waiting for the captain's expert assessment.

The captain composed himself, and managed a craggy smile. He shrugged. "Frank. Strange things happen in a fire."

Kathy dried and placed the last of her dishes on the shelf. She had washed every cup and dish by hand after first completing the unpleasant task of cleaning the refrigerator of its putrefying contents. She leaned against the counter of her U-shaped kitchen while she penned her grocery list, writing the words "*cheese*" and "*cottage*" and "*cheddar*" and finally "*Swiss*."

She stopped. She was back on the road by the lake, picturing the destroyed restaurant — the cute little chalet. And she remembered her dream. Her vision snapped back, the word "*Swiss*" in sharp focus. She slowly looked up, her eyes passing over the hard wood floor, the lower cabinets below the sink, the junk drawer. It appeared to be glowing. She walked slowly across the kitchen to the chosen drawer. There, folded in thirds, was her golden ticket, the fire insurance inspection document, just as she had dreamed it. Opening it, she flipped over the first two stapled pages and scanned down the last page to the bottom. She saw the inspector's signature and read the words aloud.

"Policy effective date: October 12, 2003. Those bastards! They *knew* we were covered!"

She began looking for Frank, paper in hand. Outside the back door she scanned the blackened slope behind the jumbled branches and spotted a young fireman digging around the burning oak that almost killed her. She walked out through the thick, pale yellow carpet of grass between herself and the branches and stopped just inside of them. "Have you seen my husband?" she called to the young man.

"Him and the captain went around to the front, Ma'am." He

said, pointing out the two small figures down at the northwest corner.

It was from this fresh angle that Kathy noticed something new. Something odd. Very odd. It appeared that some of their property had burned after all. She paused at the gate of an animal pen and stared uphill at the only area on her entire acreage that was blackened. A barren, 80' x 40' plot. She peered at it as if to decipher the mystery. Why would this one area have burned when all the rest did not? Of course, she reflected, she had no idea why the rest of her property *hadn't* burned. She looked around and took a deep breath. *What is going on around here?*

MIRACLES

Seeing is not believing. This is the first thing to get clear in talking about miracles. Whatever experiences we may have, we shall not regard them as miraculous if we already hold a philosophy which excludes the supernatural.

C.S. LEWIS

Joni, Danielle, Juliette and I were 60 miles away and hadn't seen any of the evidence that Kathy and Frank were walking through, yet we believed. Kathy's brief description over the telephone of what she had seen on her property had answered our every doubt. God had given Joni and Danielle detailed answers to very specific prayers and his answer had been a resounding yes. But how could we be so sure about it? And why were Kathy and Frank so reluctant to believe what their own eyes were telling them? The answer is simple. We believed in the supernatural. Frank and Kathy did not.

I had seen God answer many of my prayers before the Cedar Fire. And I had observed Joni's prayers being answered so often that I sometimes thought of her as a supernatural conduit. My answered prayers had been small—personal requests of a modest size that came true before my eyes. Little things. My sweet treasured evidences of God's existence seemed to me to be big enough. I believed God's time for astoundingly large physical miracles had passed — that these quiet, minor, supernatural wonders were as good as it got nowadays. Living Water? God only passed it out in tiny Dixie cups.

Joni had been frustrated — exasperated on that Monday morning, October 27, 2003. She had just watched our non-believing friends drive back toward Cuyamaca without any realistic hope of their home's survival. She had spent so much time and effort trying to help Kathy see the truth of eternal things. For years, Joni had shared as best she could about the spiritual warfare which goes on constantly all around us, and about the terrifying consequences of denying Jesus a place in your heart. But Kathy remained unconvinced. *What does it take, Lord? How can I let them know what I know about You?* So Joni drank down her tiny cup full of Living Water — the modern day Christian's customary and self-imposed limit. Then she did something very unusual. She asked the Lord for more. Much more.

"A miracle! Kathy and Frank need a miracle, Lord! It's got to be big — *so* big there isn't any explanation besides You! Show them, God!"

It had happened so fast. Her prayer was spontaneous — like running off the end of a high dive without first checking the pool for water. Neither Joni nor Danielle had planned the prayers that came effortlessly out of them in the midst of their tear-filled anguish. The bold words given to each of them seemed so far-fetched in their *own* minds that they came with a measure of surprise.

Far-fetched indeed...

When I found out what my wife and daughter had prayed for I was quite skeptical. I didn't question their sincerity, but they might as well have asked God for the ability to walk on water. On second thought, that might have required *less* supernatural intervention.

Search your memory for your closest encounter with dangerous and uncontrollable fire. Do you remember your fearful impressions? Its terrifying sights and sounds? Its searing heat? Its unpredictable advance? What on earth could save someone, or some *place* from complete and utter destruction as a raging firestorm passed directly over it? Nothing could. Yet, even in such grave circumstances the merciless flames have their master...

One day Moses was tending the flock of his father-in-law, Jethro, the priest of Midian. He led the flock far into the wilderness and came to Sinai, the mountain of God. There the angel of the Lord appeared to him in a blazing fire from the middle of a bush. Moses stared in amazement. Though the bush was engulfed in flames, it didn't burn up. "This is amazing," Moses said to himself. "Why isn't that bush burning up? I must go see it."

(Exodus 3:1-3) NLT

RAMONA   5:40 P.M.

Kathy and Frank took a trip down to Ramona on Sunday afternoon to buy groceries and diesel for the generator. The trip demonstrated the overpowering scale of the Cedar Fire's fury. The pines on the steep 1,000 foot drop-offs that Frank navigated during his twice-daily commute had been destroyed, reduced to charred tree skeletons. After they finished shopping, Frank broke the somber silence.

"Kathy, do you think, maybe, somebody took those logs while we were at your mom's? They might have just driven up and taken them all."

Kathy shook her head. "If someone had driven up and taken that wood they would've gotten ash all over the driveway and there would've been tire tracks. Everything was neat as a pin. Don't you remember the perfect rectangle? Four inches of ash where the logs used to be? Nobody touched it before we came back."

It was dark by the time they got home. Frank drove through the gate and turned right, close to the barn. Kathy saw the white pumper and the Texas fire crew gathered around a campfire in the middle of the sooted field to the south of them. The firemen had settled in for a chilly overnight stay. She noticed a small pile of wood sitting close to the fire, enough for hours of campfire storytelling. She hit the button for the window and heard one of the firemen making lovely music —

he was playing the harmonica.

The couple unloaded the groceries, then Frank loaded his wheelbarrow with two five-gallon containers full of diesel and rolled them to the pump house. He refueled the generator and started it up.

Comforted by the fire crew standing by outside, Frank and Kathy got cozy on the sofa. "I called my mom on the cell phone when you were buying diesel today. She's bringing the kids up in the morning. I hope they don't have trouble at the checkpoint."

"Frankie has his student I.D. in his wallet. That should get them through," said Frank. Then he tried out his newest fire theory on her.

"Kath, If conditions were just right, it might explain those branches not burning. Maybe the logs acted like a wind screen."

"Frank. You're driving me crazy with your stolen wood theory, your Indian hunting grounds theory, now a wind screen theory? Give it a rest."

Frank frowned. He was driving *himself* crazy with his theories. Nothing he had come up with provided a satisfactory explanation.

Later, Frank walked outside to the pump house and flipped off the generator for the night. All was quiet. He gazed up into the heavens and was awestruck by the expanse of it. Suddenly, he felt stripped of all pretension.

Diplomas, accomplishments, for what? A hundred years from now who would know that I ever existed?

He stood between the pump house and his home, staring at the countless stars. Billions of randomly constructed gigantic balls of flaming gas, thousands of light years away.

Just then, the unmistakable sound of male laughter rang out throughout the shallow valley between the peaks. It was the Texas firemen. Frank envied them. They hung out with their buddies, ate meals together, and when they did their job, the rewards were instant. Lives and homes were saved in the process.

A fireman always knows when he makes a difference, thought Frank.

He walked back into the darkened house, climbed the staircase and entered his bedroom. Kathy was in dreamless slumber. Frank put on his pajamas and slid quietly into bed. Two minutes later he was fast asleep.

8:30 A.M.

Just as the Scalaris finished a breakfast of cinnamon scones and coffee, Tom Wilby came driving up to help Frank get the solar cells working again. Frank walked down the wooden stairs and met him halfway.

"Hi Tom. I'm sorry about your house."

"Thanks. Everyone's talking about your place, Frank. Nobody understands how it didn't burn. I shake my head every time I drive by it. It's miraculous! Astounding!"

The two men arrived at the banks of solar cells. As Tom inspected them he noticed something odd, something unexpected. He ran his hand over the polished glass surface of several of them and made a startling diagnosis.

"They're ruined, Frank. They're pitted—melted from the heat."

"The heat? *What* heat? Nothing burned anywhere *near* these panels," said Frank.

"I understand that. I don't see that anything burned on your property, but the cells are fried. They're useless."

Tom looked at the ground around the panels. Yellow weeds were everywhere. He looked at the house twenty feet away.

"You know, I was home until almost nine last Tuesday night. I saw huge fire over here, then my barn exploded. I barely made it out alive. I don't get it."

"Tom. Believe me. Neither do I. So now I've got to replace all the cells?"

"I'm afraid so," said Tom. "At least you've got your house."

11:15 A.M.

Grandma Tammy drove the green mini van through the green gate. Alex, sitting next to her, reached over and honked the horn. Veronica kept the camcorder rolling, but her heart was broken. Her mountain wasn't worth looking at anymore. Just over a week ago, Veronica and Frankie had taken Alex with them on horseback down the dark forest trail to Ah-ha-'Mi-Ah-ha' and the little waterfall. It had been a magical day. It was all charred history now.

170

Kathy had spoken to her children twice since returning to the mountain. Once, briefly, on Saturday, then yesterday from Ramona. She told them days ago that the forest was gone. But now, to actually be driving through all of it... the charcoaled trees, the vanished homes, the ruined lives. And then to see their miraculously preserved ranch. The Scalari kids could hardly believe it. Frankie felt something powerful. What he saw as his grandmother drove onto their property caused a beautiful sense of awe to come over him. *God did this,* a gentle voice seemed to whisper.

"Welcome home!" said Kathy.

Anna jumped to her daddy's arms from the van.

"I missed you, Daddy!"

The two large pizzas Tammy brought up for them disappeared quickly as the family sat around the family room trading fire stories. Kathy caught them up on the last two days and on the unexplainable impossibilities scattered in several places around their ranch.

"What about Chocolate, Mom? Did you ever find her?" asked Veronica.

"No, honey, we never did," said Kathy.

"I bet coyotes got her!" blurted Alex.

"*Alex!*" yelled Frank, but the damage was done.

Veronica swallowed hard. "He's right, Dad, I'm sure coyotes got her."

After lunch, Frankie, Veronica, Alex and Anna headed outside for an unsupervised tour of the oddities their parents had told them about. After kicking around in the layer of ash left at the bottom of where the stacked logs had been, Frankie and Veronica raced toward the barn. The brother and sister met a little north of it, making a pilgrimage to the wooden stool. Frankie got on his knees to be really close. He studied the seat's detail. He realized he was focused on the miraculous.

Veronica knelt down next to him. "Really weird, huh?"

It was then that she heard it. It was barely perceptible. She got up and walked in the direction of it. Frankie followed. She paused, waiting to hear it again... *Nothing.* "Oh well." She shrugged.

Just as she and Frankie began walking back to the house, she heard the muffled sound again. Veronica zeroed in on it, following it to the east side of the barn. The door to the hay bin was half open. She wrapped her fingers around the door latch.

"Chocolate?"

She opened the door slowly and peered up to the top of a five-bale-high stack of alfalfa. *Nothing there.* A mouse darted across Veronica's toes.

"What did you hear?" Frankie asked.

"I just heard a little sound. It was probably just a mouse."

Veronica closed the hay bin door.

Buk, buk, buk, ba caak!

"*Chocolate!*" Frankie and Veronica cried out together.

Veronica flung the door open. Her little black hen cocked an orange eye down at her from the top bale.

"*Chocolate! Baby! You're alive!*"

Veronica climbed two bales of alfalfa and came face to face with her precious pet. Chocolate flew up into the air, landing on Veronica's head. She gently grasped the chicken with both hands and cradled the little black hen tight to her chest. She kissed its tiny black head. Chocolate made her happiest sound of all:

Eck-eck-eck-eck.

It was the sound she made while eating earwigs.

HIDDEN TREASURE

The Green Gate

Where is the ash?

The Scalari children come home.

Why did a magnitude 10 firestorm stop on a dime?

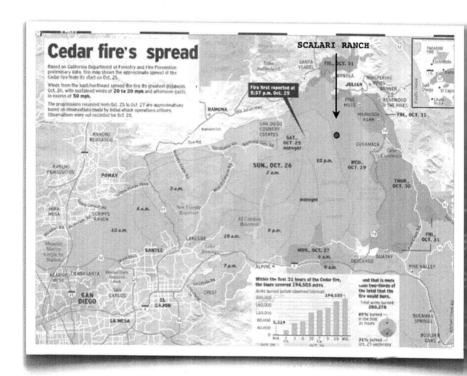

Chapter Ten
God and Fire

"When you walk through the fire, you will not be burned; the flames will not set you ablaze. For I am the Lord, your God, the Holy One of Israel, your Savior;"

(Isaiah 43:2-3)

Chapter Ten
God and Fire

NOVEMBER 2003

9:45 A.M.

Joni, Danielle, Juliette and I drove up to see the Scalari family after Highway 79 was reopened to nonresidents. Driving through what had been beautiful woods now reduced to ashes and soot was a somber experience for the four of us.

We had spotted the isolated patch of bright green from miles away on the high ridge line.

"It *was* the apple trees we saw! Girls, look!" said Joni, pointing to the shimmering orchard.

Veronica, Alex and Anna scampered down the balcony stairs at the sight of the familiar Dodge truck. Joni stopped in front of the house on the driveway near the big oak. Danielle and Juliette jumped out of the rear cab and ran to their friends waiting for them at the swing. As we drove up the dirt drive next to the house both of us immediately noticed the empty space where the massive stack of wood used to be. Frank and Kathy stepped off the back porch.

"Are you looking for the wood? It all burned up," said Kathy. Joni gave her bewildered friend a hug.

"Joni, I don't know what to make of all this. Let me show you." Kathy walked us to underneath the intruding oak branch.

"Look at this. The tree stopped burning where this branch came over my property! How could it do that?"

"God, Kathy. God did this. This was my prayer for you. It was Danielle's, too. God answered our prayers. That's what we're looking at. God is real. Don't you see that now?"

All Frank could do was smile. "I still can't make any sense of it."

We drifted over to the still-existing branches. Brown pine needles, inches thick, lay on the ground all around the messy pile. The unburned ground turned to black soot and gray ash in a sharp demarcation all along the back side of them.

"How could *this* happen?" Kathy asked.

Joni smiled at her, not answering for long seconds. Juliette high-pitched giggle rang out from the swing in the front of the house.

"God did this, Kathy. God did all of this."

"But Joni! Our neighbor's houses all burned to the ground! Why would He save our property and let theirs burn? Yesterday we watched a car pull up outside the gate and just sit there. I recognized the woman. Her husband stopped the car for her to look. Their home burned to the ground just up the mountain from us. She had the nastiest look on her face. She sat there and scowled at us for the longest time."

"It's not that He let the other homes burn, Kathy. It's that He answered our prayers for *your* property."

We walked into the midst of the apple orchard.

"The air smells sweet around us," Joni said. "I don't smell the fire." She wrapped her hand around a branch from an apple tree and began rubbing the leaves between her thumb and forefinger. She brought her hand to her nose and sniffed. "No smoke! My fingers smell like apples! Amazing!"

I scanned the property, "There's no ash. *Anywhere*."

"I was waiting for you to notice," said Frank. "The fire insurance company sent an adjuster out a few days ago to look around. She cut us a check for all the cleanup we obviously did, but I told her that we never cleaned up. There wasn't anything to clean."

Danielle took a running start toward the swing and jumped to a standing position on the wood plank seat. She swung forward, rising ten feet into the air before reaching the end of the long arc. She came to a stop. Danielle could see the barn and the black field to the south of it. She glanced at Neo and Cindy munching apples in the orchard. Just as she began to swing backwards, she looked to her left. *Strange,* she thought. Now she was curious. Danielle got off the swing and walked up the dirt driveway to the south side of the house. She turned around and focused her vision down to where the road began —down to the green gate. She followed the dirt driveway past the chicken coop, alongside the sooty field to the south, and parallel to the big oak with the swing. What she saw made no sense at all. Not to a nine-year-old, not to a 49-year old. The vast blackened field to her left had been completely burned. Well, almost completely. A strange finger of clumpy yellow weeds still remained. It was a 20-foot-long peninsula of straw-colored grass.

Why? Danielle wondered.

Juliette came over to see. "What're you doing?"

"Julie, *look!*" She pointed to the yellow peninsula of weeds surrounded on three sides by acres of black ground.

"Therefore once more I will astound these people with wonder upon wonder: the wisdom of the wise will perish, the intelligence of the intelligent will vanish."

(Isaiah 29:14)

Kathy, Frank, Joni and I sat around the dining room table making friendly small talk while drinking Kathy's Serena Organic coffee. We were marking time before pondering the imponderable. Then the "elephant in the room" raised its trunk. I suppose I helped it along...

"What do you think happened here the night of the fire, Frank? Why didn't your property burn?"

"I wasn't here, Greg. I really don't know. There *is* an explanation, but I can't explain it. What do *you* believe happened that night?"

"Look. I'm a gas serviceman. I had to jump through hoops to become certified. My main area of expertise may surprise you. Flame characteristics. I'm highly trained in what fire is, how it works, and what it needs. Wildfires create wind, Frank. They pull in air from all directions to fuel their flames, but no embers flew in here at all. 100-foot-flames burned through a stack of logs a few feet from this house and had no effect? Impossible. C'mon Mr. Science, *you* know the laws of thermodynamics. The evidence is overwhelming. If you and Kathy had been here with Chocolate that night you'd have seen signs and wonders in progress all over your property. What do *you* think Kathy?"

Kathy shrugged. "Oh, I don't know, Greg. I guess we were lucky. *Very* lucky. I've always been lucky. Even when I was a kid. We had some neighbors come by. Tom and Sharon Wilby. They live down the road. Well, I mean they *used* to live down the road. Their house and barn and everything else burned to the ground. Anyway, a few weeks before the fire the two of them came over and introduced themselves. Sharon told me about this part of the mountain being Indian hunting grounds hundreds of years ago. We've even found grinding holes behind us in a rock near some oak trees. Frank believes we live on land sacred to the Indians. Maybe that's why it wouldn't burn."

"Those Indians must've had mighty small hunting grounds." I said. "What about your neighbors? They all lived on the hunting grounds, too. And, even *if* dead Indians had that power, it surely would be supernatural."

Joni had been waiting her turn. "*God* was here that terrible night! He protected your property as the fire raged all around it. He didn't even let any ash or smoke come in! Can't you two see that?"

Frankie sat quietly, not saying a word. That had always been his way. He listened, always listened. He would not give his opinion unless you asked him for it, then he would tell you what he believed in as few words as possible. As soon as he finished Frankie would return to listening. I read something in his eyes as Joni debated the natural versus the supernatural with his parents. It was a softening, a craving for the truth no matter where the truth led him.

Frank looked incredulous. "You two actually believe God came down onto our property and just told the flames, 'No, not this one?'"

"That's exactly what Joni and I believe." I had just the Old Testament story to prove it, too. I walked out to the truck and retrieved my Bible. I sat back down at the dining table next to Joni and thumbed through to the middle of the book.

"I want to tell both of you a story. It's from the older part of the Bible, the part written down before Jesus was born. Is that all right with both of you? It isn't very long."

"Sure, go ahead," said Frank.

Kathy nodded her agreement.

I put a ribbon in the third chapter of Daniel and closed the book.

"Six hundred years before Christ was born, Israel had been defeated and forced into captivity by the Babylonians," I began. "King Nebuchadnezzar chose four Jewish teenagers to be groomed to serve him. The king renamed the teens. Daniel became known as Belteshazzar, and his three friends became Shadrach, Meshach and Abednego. Each of them were given responsibilities inside the royal government. The young men pleased the king with honest work and trustworthy character, but unknown to him, each day the boys continued praying and worshipping their God. Years later, King Nebuchadnezzar commissioned an image of gold to be built for himself. It was 90 feet high and 9 feet wide. They set it up on a place called the plain of Dura. It's a real place south of Baghdad, Iraq today. The king decreed that all his government officials and all the people in Babylon would come to the dedication of his golden image. When everyone was standing before it, the king gave this one simple rule of worship: 'Whenever the king's band strikes up the music, you will fall on your face and worship my golden image, because if you don't, you'll immediately be thrown into the blazing furnace.' This outdoor furnace was huge, Frank. It had a winding set of steps to the top of it. They'd tie up the king's enemies, carry them up to the top and shove them through the flue – the opening at the top. They'd fall into the middle of the blazing flames below where the king had a special viewing slot at the bottom to watch."

"When does this guy, Daniel, show up?" Frank wondered.

"He doesn't. Daniel must've been out of the country that day, but Shadrach, Meshach and Abednego were there, and they watched the dedication along with the other government officials, including the king's astrologers who loathed Jews in general, but *really* hated these 'palace Jews' because they were Nebuchadnezzar's favorites. I think the astrologers must've watched to see if these three guys trusted their God enough to burn for him. The three friends stood praying silently while they listened to horrifying details of being roasted alive in the blazing furnace. Nebuchadnezzar gave the band leader his cue and the strange music began. All the government officials, the prefects, the princes, captains of the army, the judges, the king's advisers — Shadrach, Meshach and Abednego were in that group — and all those in the great crowd gathered out on the plain of Dura began taking comfort in the mass humiliation. The astrologers grudgingly began to bow down but kept their eyes locked upon the 'palace Jews' four rows in front of them. What they saw must've filled their evil hearts with glee. Shadrach, Meshach and Abednego were not bowing. These three men alone remained upright amid hundreds of thousands of people prostrating themselves to the king's golden image. Instead, these Jewish believers stood praying silently to God. The young men weren't afraid.

The king squinted in the afternoon sunshine, shading his eyes with his hand as he peered into his royal gallery of government bureaucrats. With the anxious help of the chief astrologer, the king spotted the three of them. He became furious when he realized that these were three of the four Jewish men he had rescued from the miserable conditions the rest of his slaves endured. 'Bring Shadrach, Meshach and Abednego to me now!' the king commanded.

So the three of them were brought quickly to stand before the king, and as he watched them being dragged roughly up the steps into his presence, his affection for them returned. He had decided to give them another chance. He would grant them pardon if they bowed in front of him to his golden image. Shadrach, Meshach and Abednego stood at attention before Nebuchadzezzar, showing all due respect to the most powerful man in the world. The looks on their faces must've puzzled the king. He could've seen it in their eyes. They were serene, relaxed, and strangest of all, they were confident, as if they knew something that he didn't.

The king spoke to them. 'Is it true, Shadrach, Meshach and Abednego, that you do not serve my gods or worship the image of gold I have set up? Now when you hear the sound of the music, if you are ready to fall down and worship the image I made, very good. But if you do *not* worship it, you will be thrown immediately into the blazing furnace. Then what god will be able to rescue you from my hand?'"

I walked to the kitchen for more coffee. Frank followed after me.

"What about the end of the story? Do they get thrown into the furnace?" he asked.

"I'd like to read the rest of the story to you right out of the Bible. Is that okay with you?"

"Yes, it's a good fable. I'd like to hear how it ends," said the physicist.

When Frank and I returned to the table, Joni and Kathy were in the middle of their *own* Bible study:

"But Joni, how do you know that Nebuchadnezzar or his statue, or his palace ever existed? Somebody could've made the whole thing up."

"I'll take that one," I said. "In the eighties, Saddam Hussein rebuilt Nebuchadnezzar's palace right on top of its ancient foundation on the plain of Dura, the very spot where this story took place. They rebuilt it using thousands of bricks from the ancient palace ruins. Every twenty-six-hundred-year-old brick that was found had the name 'Nebuchadnezzar' pressed into it. Now, shall I read you the end of the story?"

I began to read from Daniel:

Shadrach, Meshach and Abednego replied to him, "King Nebuchadnezzar, we do not need to defend ourselves before you in this matter. If we are thrown into the blazing furnace, the God we serve is able to deliver us from us from Your Majesty's hand. But even if he does not, we want you to know, Your Majesty, that we will not serve your gods or worship the image of gold you have set up."

Then Nebuchadnezzar was furious with Shadrach, Meshach and Abednego, and his attitude toward them changed. He ordered the furnace heated seven times hotter than usual and commanded some of the strongest soldiers in his army to tie up Shadrach, Meshach and

Abednego and throw them into the blazing furnace. So these men, wearing their robes, trousers, turbans and other clothes, were bound and thrown into the blazing furnace. The king's command was so urgent and the furnace was so hot that the flames of the fire killed the soldiers who took up Shadrach, Meshach and Abednego, and these three men, firmly tied, fell into the blazing furnace.

Then King Nebuchadnezzar leaped to his feet in amazement and asked his advisers, "Weren't there three men that we tied up and threw into the fire?"

They replied, "Certainly, Your Majesty."

He said, "Look! I see four men walking around in the fire, unbound and unharmed, and the fourth looks like a son of the gods."

Nebuchadnezzar then approached the opening of the blazing furnace and shouted, "Shadrach, Meshach and Abednego, servants of the Most High God, come out! Come here!"

So Shadrach, Meshach and Abednego came out of the fire, and the satraps, prefects, governors and royal advisers crowded around them. They saw that the fire had not harmed their bodies, nor was a hair of their heads singed; their robes were not scorched, and there was no smell of fire on them.

Then Nebuchadnezzar said, "Praise be to the God of Shadrach, Meshach and Abednego, who has sent his angel and rescued his servants! They trusted in him and defied the king's command and were willing to give up their lives rather than serve or worship any other god except their own God. Therefore I decree that the people of any nation or language who say anything against the God of Shadrach, Meshach and Abednego be cut to into pieces and their houses be turned into piles of rubble, for no other god can save in this way."

(Daniel 3:16-30)

I closed my Bible. "*That*, is what I believe happened here that night. Not only were Shadrach, Meshach, Abednego and their garments unburned, they didn't even smell like fire. Does this sound familiar?"

I stared at Frank and Kathy. They stared right back at me.

186

"Greg. We've been over this before," said Frank.

We had indeed. One of the things I treasured about my friendship with Frank was that we could speak honestly and openly with one another about our beliefs. We had been around and around about the authority of the Bible, the divinity of Jesus Christ, the existence of a personal God who loved us. We had sliced and diced the arguments for hours, always arriving at a standstill.

This time something different was going on, however. I was willing to debate the issues again, but I knew in my heart we were sitting smack dead center in the middle of a miracle. That's what I wanted to keep in focus. I could feel God's power.

"That's true," I said. "But we've never discussed any of those things while sitting in the middle of a miracle. This is beyond explanation. You two have to see that."

"How can you explain it?" Joni asked.

Frank and Kathy nodded. Frank never minced words. He was honest. "You're right. Something happened here. And I can't explain it. I'll give you that much."

Later that afternoon, our two families ate barbecued chicken and potato salad together. At sunset we had a campfire. After the last marshmallow had been toasted Frank and I were left to ourselves. We sat around the small fire in an old wash tub out in front of the house. I dropped in a log and watched the bright bed of coals at the bottom quickly catch it aflame. The two of us sat there on opposite sides of the same fire, the quiet between us broken by sharp cracks and pops. We were at a spiritual standoff. Frank broke the silence.

"Greg, infinite, unified truth doesn't exist," he said. "Or if it does, science hasn't discovered it. No one has all the answers, not a god, and not a man. The universe is an untidy place. It's messy— quirky on the molecular level. The ultimate truth is that there *is* no ultimate truth. No pure good and no pure evil. Only empty space between positive and negative subatomic charges. Whether a person's character embraces one polarity or the other makes little difference, ultimately. Each ends up in the same condition: dead."

"Okay then. In your scientific opinion, what happens when we die, Doc?"

Frank stared into the flames. High on the summit of Poco

187

Montana a coyote's cry pierced the evening's chill, breaking Frank's hypnotic gaze. "Once exhausted of life energy," he said, "each living body, human or otherwise, becomes inert, like a car battery drained of its charge, but the energy of the life form continues on into the cosmos. Energy changes form, but it never really disappears."

"Then what about prayers? How do they get answered? And if they *do*, who answers them?"

"Paranormal activity is a scientific fact, Greg. It is measurable. Joni seems to be a lightning rod for it. If a flurry of paranormal activity occurred on my property during the fire, a god is responsible."

"God is responsible?" I was overjoyed at hearing the word come from his lips.

"Yes, a god, but not the god of the Bible. This god is in the rocks, the trees and the plants. It is inside of everything on earth, but it is an energy force, not an all-knowing and all-seeing director. Joni and Danielle's paranormal requests tapped into this extraordinary force like the Indians used to. I congratulate them."

Frank, if you and Kathy had been here with Chocolate that night as this mountain burned down and you had watched God's signs and wonders in progress all over your property while sitting here on this very spot, if you had seen the wind raging outside your property but not a breath of wind, not an ember blowing in right here where you're sitting, if you could've walked right up to your side of the engulfed tree trunks as 200-foot-high flames raged a few feet from your house and felt no heat, then would you have believed?"

A slight smile formed at a corner of Frank's mouth. He appeared to be enjoying the possibility of my argument if not swallowing it.

"Doc, do you remember being a kid and taking a magnifying glass outside on a warm, sunny day?"

"You're all over the map."

"I know, I know. Indulge me for a minute. Imagine you're eight again. Picture yourself in front of that jumbled up pile of kindling over there behind the house. You've got a large magnifying glass and it's a warm sunny day."

Frank stared dispassionately at me.

"You quickly recognize the pine needles as the easiest fuel. You make a little pile, then you work the position of the concentrated sunlight onto a spot in the needles. After a minute or so, you produce an ember. Then, with the help of some air from your lungs, a flicker of flame emerges in the dry kindling. Soon, combustion wind is flowing from all directions, even through the needles that aren't burning. Two minutes later the entire pile of branches is roaring with fire."

Frank closed his eyes. He imagined himself at 8-years-old, standing in front of the flaming pile of kindling. He visualized the C-130 he'd seen on the freeway. It swooped low over his head and dropped a full load of red fire retardant all over little Frank and his fire.

"Now let's take 8-year-old Frank over to the stacked tree trunks, twelve feet away. Have him train his concentrated sunlight on one of the cut ends of the logs. We can leave him out there until lunch — until sunset if we want to, but he isn't going to catch that any of those logs on fire. The fuel is too dense and his source of ignition isn't powerful enough. Yet, your kindling is still sitting over there behind your house, Doc, and all your tree trunks are gone. You see the problem?"

"Greg, *believe* me, I see the problem, but I can't come to your conclusion. I *can't*. I wasn't here. Maybe if I had seen it happening with my own eyes."

I felt a deep sadness as I listened to my friend defend his disbelief. Frank was spiritually blind. I could testify to my baptism in the Spirit one Sunday in early January 1985, I could review the historical reality of Jesus, and that Christ was proclaimed as Savior in every book of the Old Testament, I could use my expertise in flame characteristics to tell Frank technical reasons why a wildfire could never do what it did in the very place where we were sitting, but it was all gibberish to Frank. I realized right then that many of the people in the towns where Jesus had walked had known the blind man, the paralytic, or the leper from the time they were children. Jesus had healed their friend in front of them but they still would not believe. I felt like a spiritual 'Christopher Columbus' who showed up after being mistakenly invited to The Flat Earth Society Picnic: "The Earth is round, I tell you! *Round!*"

Later that evening we said our goodbyes and headed home. For Danielle, Juliette, Joni and I, the afterglow of such a momentous day tasted sweet, but it was tinged with an undeniable melancholy. That morning we had tread upon the very ground God's Spirit had hovered upon just over a week ago. We had sat upon furniture and conversed inside rooms which could not possibly have survived the flames. Yet they did. Tonight, Frank was tucking little Anna into her impossible bed. In the morning, Kathy would cook the family breakfast on her miraculous stove. In spite of it all, our friends remained unconvinced. This was not the outcome Joni and I had envisioned. Our hearts ached for the Scalari family. It was as if Kathy and Frank had been given the map to a thick vein of pure gold a few inches below their apple trees and had dismissed it as a hoax.

I knew the middle of the county had just burned down. I knew thousands of people were homeless. I could only imagine the pain and suffering of the families who lost loved ones in the fire. But what we had just seen in the middle of the destroyed Cuyamaca Mountains made me want to shout from the rooftops! I felt like Jimmy Stewart as George Bailey given a second chance in "It's a Wonderful Life." I wanted to rush out into the streets of San Diego screaming: "He is real! God is *real!* He was here! Right *here!"*

God hadn't disguised the evidence of his supernatural intervention, it was obvious to see right out there in the sunlight. And the Lord didn't seem to be constrained by any particular denomination's doctrine about the size of the miracles God does and does *not* do during the Church Age. God *is* God, after all.

I glanced over at Joni on the other side of the dark truck cab. She had fallen asleep on the long ride home. Likewise for the girls strapped in behind me. I looked back to the lonely mountain road and the black starry sky broken only by twin shafts of light from my high beams. I sat there in the driver's seat, alone in my thoughts, and I reflected on the gigantic faith of Shadrach, Meshach and Abednego before being thrown into the fiery furnace. I couldn't help but think of Joni. Only three people in a crowd of one million had the type of resolute belief necessary to stand up for God that day. If Joni had been there I was quite certain there would've been four. It occurred to me that her type of belief couldn't be willed or taught, it had to be a gift from God. Apparently, it has always been quite rare. I certainly didn't have it. Could it be possible that the short supply of such a courageous belief is the reason we do not see more awe-inspiring manifestations of God's sovereign power today?

Joni had deserved someone so much better than me. I was only a marginal believer the day we were married. I was in the music business at the time as a soundman and manager for a popular bar band and Joni was my roadie — the cutest little roadie a man could imagine.

A year later her father came to visit. Joni warned me that he never missed a Sunday without a sitting on a pew, so I reluctantly agreed to go to my drummer's Baptist church.

There I was, sitting front and center between Joni and her dad and listening to everyone around me sing to God. As I listened to the worship music, I sensed something special happening. There was a kind of loving devotion filling the room. Suddenly, it came to me. I had been the ungrateful recipient of such a beautiful devotion. Joni had given it to me. She had been the Christlike influence in my self-absorbed life. This was her source. God was her answer. She had always told me so, but until right then I hadn't understood. I was overcome with great emotion.

Two Sundays later I raised my hand.

By taking a long and thoughtful look at what God has created, people have always been able to see what their eyes as such can't see: eternal power, for instance, and the mystery of his divine being. So nobody has a good excuse. What happened was this: People knew God perfectly well, but when they didn't treat him like God, refusing to worship him, they trivialized themselves into silliness and confusion so that there was neither sense nor direction left in their lives. They pretended to know it all, but were illiterate regarding life. They traded the glory of God who holds the whole world in his hands for cheap figurines you can buy at any roadside stand.

(Romans 1:20-23) MSG

Shadrach, Meshack and Abednego In the Fiery Furnace painted 300 A.D. Inside the ancient Catacombs of Rome

The Scalari's ranch from the air, 12-06-03.

House

Big oak & swing

Barn

Apple Orchard

193

Chapter Eleven
Last Pieces

For the word of God is living and active. Sharper than any double-edged sword, it penetrates even to dividing soul and spirit, joints and marrow. It judges the thoughts and attitudes of the heart.

(Hebrews 4:12)

Chapter Eleven
Last Pieces

THE DIVING BOARD

QUITE A WHILE after the fire, Kathy accepted a Bible as a gift from Joni and me. She called one day and unknowingly put my newly discovered belief in the Lord's absolute sovereignty to the test. I picked up the phone...

"Greg, if I ask God a question will He answer it? Can I just close my eyes, ask my question, and open my Bible?" Kathy asked.

This practice is sometimes referred to as "Magic 8 ball" theology. It is not recommended. But, Kathy was genuinely asking me about the Lord for the first time. She wanted to know if this God we had been telling her about for so long could answer her question straight out of His book. In this instance, I was sure that the Lord was in charge of the timing of Kathy's call and of her unsteady small leap of faith toward Him. I certainly wasn't going to shut her sliver of light off by playing it safe. To me, these "now or never" moments of faith resemble most closely a trip out to the edge of a diving board: *Do I jump, or don't I? Do I trust the water to break my fall?*

A good analogy except the water Kathy and I are about to leap into is Living Water, and this water is invisible. I got out on the diving board of my faith and determined that we would jump. Would there be any living water at the bottom? I couldn't see any, but that is how it always happens out here within the power of the Holy Spirit. You either jump, or God takes you off the board. If that happens, you may never get the opportunity to go out there again.

"Yes, Kathy, you surely can, and He surely will."

"I've got my Bible right here. Can I just open it and begin reading?" she asked.

"Go ahead."

And so...we jumped. I realized that within the next few seconds Kathy would either be swimming within His living water or *not*.

What if she flips the Bible open to an obscure genealogy, I thought. *Or a harsh but deserved condemnation of some godless Baal worshippers? What will I say to her?*

Yet, I had yielded control of the situation to Christ because Jesus is the one who placed me within it. I reflected that it was Christ's outcome, not mine. *Your words, not my words, prepare the soil, Lord. Let's go!*

On my end of the phone, I heard a few moments of silence, then whispered screams of amazement. Kathy's eyes had focused on four incredible words she had blindly pointed to in the middle of Nehemiah 9:25.

"Oh my God! Listen to the words above my finger!"

"fruit trees in abundance..."

Kathy read the pages before and after this small fragment of God's Word and was astounded by God's answer to her leap of faith in Him. In this area of Scripture, God is reminding the Israelites of the many times He had forgiven them their rebellion, their disobedience, their awful blasphemies, their disbelief and lack of trust. He is reminding them of how he has delivered them in miraculous ways time after time when they cried out to Him.

But you are a forgiving God, gracious and compassionate, slow to anger and abounding in love.

(Nehemiah 9:17)

The Word of the Lord filled Kathy with fear and joy that day as God spoke to her heart in a personal way, cutting through her doubts and confirming to her that it was God alone that had saved her property. She had been given the perfect Scripture as she struggled to make sense of the impossible reality of an entire five acre property that would not burn, and while the word 'fruit' or the phrase 'bearing fruit' are scattered here and there throughout the Bible, references to 'fruit trees,' as in an orchard, are very rare. In fact, in the New International Version of the Bible, Nehemiah 9:25 contains one of the only references to a grouping of trees similar to the Scalari's apple orchard. Kathy's personal experience with God in the Old Testament Book of Nehemiah was unexpected, but I explained to her that The Word is like a multifaceted diamond which reveals different dazzling colors from different personal angles.

SHEEP VERSES GOATS

Many of the details within the mosaic of miracles contained within the Scalari's property became known to Joni and me much later after conversing with Kathy over a long period of time. The plastic bags on the landing, for example. This, the most instantly understandable impossibility, was a revelation to me when Kathy gave us her account of them shortly before I began work on this book. The burned goat pen was another. In my mind, nothing at all burned on their property that night. That is what I understood and that is what I wanted to be true.

When Kathy, Joni, and I first watched the video Veronica had shot the day she first came home, I was very surprised when the camera panned behind the power house and onto the burned animal pen. Frankly, I was disappointed. By the time we visited Kathy and Frank's place in mid-November, 2003, the goats were back in their pen and had erased the sooted ground inside of it.

God, I was sure that nothing at all had burned on their property, I thought, while watching the contrary evidence play in front of me. I kept replaying the video of the burned goat pen. Weeks went by without an understanding of why just this one area burned completely. It didn't make sense to me. Goats eat everything they can get their teeth on. There were no trees within the pen. There weren't even any weeds. Yet the fire blackened the entire ground within it, which was all bare dirt. The areas on either side of the pen were covered with dry weeds but were untouched by the flames. Could the fire that blackened the bare dirt of this fenced pen have crept downhill from beyond the eastern property line? Fire travels easily going uphill, not downhill. This was especially likely to be true due to the scant fuel for the flames inside this 40 foot by 80 foot enclosure. Could it have been that the fire roared through the Scalari's entire five-acre property that night but wasn't allowed to destroy anything until the flames climbed uphill into this one area?

I struggled for several weeks with the meaning of the sooted goat enclosure, the darkest piece of God's miracle mosaic. The rest of the miracles in His fire puzzle had been relatively easy to understand. The blackened goat pen was the counterpoint to them. It was a mind blowing, upside down, inside out, black is white and white is black bit of antimatter.

No fuel? Bare ground? No problem for God! The dirt caught fire! I thought.

All I could do was to tell God that I didn't understand and ask Him to help me.

Close to a month went by before Kathy and the kids dropped by for a visit. I began taking Kathy back to the days after the fire. Joni and I talked with her over coffee as we sat around our kitchen table, and I brought up the video clip that Kathy, Joni, and I first watched together the day she brought it to us on a disc a month earlier. She had been surprised along with us when she saw the blackened pen. She had forgotten about seeing it three years earlier.

"Kathy, the pen that burned, what did the previous homeowners use it for?" I asked.

"They kept goats in there like we do. Why?"

I picked up my Bible. "I remember something about goats. Sheep and goats. I think it's in one of the gospels."

I checked the NIV concordance for the word "goats" and found seven Scriptures listed. Matthew 25:32 is about separating the sheep from the goats. I read this verse to Kathy:

"All the nations will be gathered before him, and he will separate the people one from another as a shepherd separates the sheep from the goats. He will put the sheep on his right and the goats on his left. Then the King will say to those on his right, 'Come, you who are blessed by my Father; take your inheritance, the kingdom prepared for you since the creation of the world."

(Matthew 25:32-34)

"I remember this Scripture now," I said. "We're either in the sheep column, or we're in the goat column. Kathy, let me tell you, no one will want to be separated into the goat column by Jesus on that day. Listen to this:

"Then he will say to those on his left, 'Depart from me, you who are cursed, into the eternal fire prepared for the devil and his angels.'"

(Matthew 25:41)

Goose bumps rose on her arms as I read. The meaning of the blackened goat enclosure was clear to me now. Within the context of His other miracles on the Scalari's property, this one was a warning. This visage was the teeth in God's law. God had not saved the *'place of the goats'* from destruction. Goats are God's chosen illustration for those of us who will not recognize the voice of Christ, our Great Shepherd, or accept the free gift of His grace. Another piece of His perfect and supernatural mosaic slipped into place.

LAST PIECES

The goat pen

The northern property line (fence) shows the trunks of the green oak trees beyond beyond the goat pen.

Neo   Elise

BEARING WITNESS-GOD INSIDE THE FIRE

I began telling people God's beautiful story one day in January 2004. I was on the job, setting gas meters in a new housing tract when I saw a familiar face. It was Mahoney, the big, African-American site manager for a homebuilder. The man was in joyful tears after I finished telling him the details of God's recent fiery miracles in the Cuyamacas. Mahoney's strong reaction to the story started me on a Spirit-filled quest. That spring, Joni watched me share God's story in front of hundreds of people at our church. Soon, I was telling the story every day. By 2006, I was telling the story more than once a day. New miracles began happening as I told it. I began receiving what I came to understand to be divine appointments with strangers throughout my work day. Sometimes I would walk into a customer's home to figure out why the furnace wouldn't work, then a lonely widow, or a brokenhearted young man would begin to tell me their story. As the Spirit led me, I would ask the person if they were a believer.

"I believe in God, there must be something up there," was the typical response.

"Do you remember the Cedar Fire?" was always my next question.

"Oh yes, what a terrible fire. Couldn't breathe for days. Then all that ash."

"I've got a story about a miracle that happened during the Cedar Fire. Would you like to hear it?" Then I would tell them God's story while I worked. Reactions to it ranged from joy to fear, and from terror to amazement. Goose bumps rose and tears flowed.

One particular woman shook in fear as I testified to the miracles.

"Ma'am? Are you all right?" She stood quaking like a leaf.

"God is real! God is *real!*" cried the woman.

"Yes, Ma'am. God is real," I said.

People loved every miraculous detail of the miracles, and I loved watching their faces light up as it dawned on many of them for the very first time that God is real, that God is sovereign, and that even the towering flames of the Cedar Fire had to obey him.

Some years later it became apparent to me that it was time to write it down.

Yellow peninsula south of the property line wouldn't burn. Why?

THE LAST PIECE

Whether you turn to the right or to the left, your ears will hear a voice behind you, saying, "This is the way; walk in it."

(Isaiah 30:21)

I sat in front of my computer screen, staring at the latest chapter in progress, butting heads again with some troubling photographs. I could not make sense of them. I took another look at the photos taken after the fire, closely examining those I couldn't understand. One showed the big oak in front of the house. The other showed the south side of the Scalari's house and Frankie standing on the balcony ramp. There, right in the middle of both pictures was something very strange. A mystery.

When I began work extracting photos from the video, I was compelled to retrieve these photographs as well, but I could not have told you why. I didn't like these pictures. They confused me. From the first time I watched the video of the Scalari's property that had been shot two days after Kathy and Frank returned home, I noticed a bright, unburned patch of weeds to the south of the property line. I wasn't happy about that unburned patch. It didn't appear to help my case for God being responsible for the miracles. To be honest, I believed this might serve as evidence against it. Some might say:

"See, there *is* a spot that didn't burn that wasn't within the Scalari's property. It *wasn't* just their property that remained untouched." I resented the yellow peninsula of protected weeds south of the prayed-for-property. The preserved grass seemed to argue for random chance as a viable theory for why God's treasured field didn't burn. Besides, it didn't fit my template: *The miracles happened only within the Scalari's five acres.*

At the time, I was so overjoyed at the undeniable physical evidence displayed in the other photographs that I decided the best thing to do was to simply ignore the contrary ones. I began adding the lines and text to the photographs of the area where the tree trunks had vanished and of the impossible pile of branches and then all the other photographs. I understood what I was looking at in all of them. Trees in the background of the goat pen photo remained green at the top. Why? Well, as the firestorm moved rapidly uphill it burned only the trunks and lower branches of the biggest trees. The upper halves of these trees were above height of the flames so just the lower half of them burned. I had no such understanding of the pictures of the yellow peninsula. I regularly had to push these photos to the back of my mind to keep my focus on the miracles I already understood. I wondered what I should do with these aberrant pieces of evidence. *Should I just not include them? What will I write about them? Beats me?* That couldn't be what God had in mind. I knew it would be wrong to not share the entire story, aberrant evidence and all, but I had thoughts of just omitting these photos completely to avoid confusing the reader. God's story was neat and tidy, perfect, except for that strange peninsula of high weeds that was conspicuously outside the Scalari's southern boundary. Then, one day, a small, gentle, and lovely voice whispered to me from just behind the world's curtain.

There is another one. You haven't found it, but it is there... in the pictures.

I assumed it to be just wishful thinking. I even felt a little greedy about what I thought to be my wish for even more evidence of God's grace, mercy, power, and love. Months passed as I slowly brought the book's narrative to life. Then, in a quiet and solitary moment the gentle whisper returned.

There is another one. You haven't found it, but it is there... in the pictures.

I continued revising the colored lines and text on all the other photos. When I completed them, there was still one large piece of this amazing puzzle that didn't fit. *The blackened field south of the Scalari's property. The mysterious, yellow, weed-filled peninsula south of the Scalari's line.* It confounded me. Why didn't these weeds burn up like the rest of the field? Was God's protection in effect south of the Scalari property? Why? It was just a weed choked field. It made no sense and I doubted it ever would. I would just have to move forward without ever knowing what it meant. I drew a line around the unburned area in the photo and moved on.

"Go out and stand before me on the mountain," the Lord told him. And as Elijah stood there, the Lord passed by, and a mighty windstorm hit the mountain. It was such a terrible blast that the rocks were torn loose, but the Lord was not in the wind. After the wind there was an earthquake, but the Lord was not in the earthquake. And after the earthquake there was a fire, but the Lord was not in the fire. And after the fire there was the sound of a gentle whisper.

(1 Kings 19:11-12) NLT

In the Lord's timing, the meaning of the protected area of weeds to the south of the Scalari's boundary was revealed. With this last jaw-dropping piece of evidence came the most obvious and benevolent miracle of all. The photographs were overflowing proof of the power of the Holy Spirit to accomplish each precise detail and every single word uttered in the prayers of believers—especially children, who ask and believe God can and will answer them.

He reveals deep and hidden things: he knows what lies in darkness, and light dwells with him.

(Daniel 2:22)

This was the missing piece in the Lord's mosaic of miracles, completed years earlier on the night of October 28, 2003. To understand these difficult photographs I needed to review the prayer my nine-year-old daughter, Danielle, (she's eighteen now) prayed the day the Scalaris were ferrying their children and animals to Grandma Tammy's place in Jamul, California, October 27, 2003.

DANIELLE'S PRAYER
"God! Please! Keep everything just like I remember it! Protect the house, protect the barn, protect the fruit trees and the animals! Please, Jesus! Protect the big oak in front of the house with our swing! Keep everything just like it was before the fire!"

Danielle asked that the house be protected.

"Yes."

She asked God to protect the barn.

"Check."

She asked God to protect the fruit trees.

"Done."

"Jesus, please protect the animals."

"Chocolate, you're safe."

She asked Him to keep everything just like it was before the fire.

"Was there any ash or smell of smoke or fire on that property before the fire? Then, neither shall there be any after it."

Details. God knows every one of them. In my life, and in yours. Danielle had prayed for one more thing. She prayed for:

"the big oak in front of the house with our swing."

She specifically prayed for the huge old oak tree with the idyllic scream ride of a swing. Look at the photograph on page 210. The huge old oak tree with the beloved long swing grew over the southern property line decades ago. The upper branches extend far over the line. The shadow of these branches is directly over the unburned peninsula. Now look at the photograph on page 211. This is what the scene would've looked like around 9:00 P.M., Tuesday, October 28, 2003.

In order for God to answer Danielle's specific prayer that this tree remain just like it was before the fire, His supernatural protection needed to be extended *beyond* the southern property line because the oak tree extended beyond it. If the weeds inside the reverse shadow, the yellow peninsula, had burned, part of the big oak tree with the swing would have burned with them and Danielle's prayer would not have been completely fulfilled. When God saves, He saves completely! Therefore, the yellow patch of weeds under the branches would not burn! Astounding!

The small gentle whisper returned, breaking in from beyond the curtain, but *this* time He came rejoicing.

Here is the other one! You have found it!

There are no ashes within the yellow peninsula. How is that possible? Could luck be involved? A special dead Indian force field, perhaps? Could a freaky U-shaped wind shift have pushed the advancing flames of the blazing field *away* from these bone-dry weeds? Could a different bizarre wind pattern have forced the fire's fast flowing combustion wind into right angle turns around this weed patch as it raced into 150-foot flames 20 feet away?

Every burning ember had to be prevented from entering this peninsula of yellow grass for the duration of the firestorm and for days afterward for this picture to be possible. If just one cinder or one smoldering ember of ash had intruded into the air space above the protected weeds, flames would have erupted.

A 9-year-old's tearful, begging, prayer as she sat rocking on her backyard swing, was heard and fulfilled to the *letter* by the Author of the universe.

"Click"

The last piece in the Lord's wondrous mosaic fits to perfection.

Danielle's prayed for oak with the swing extends beyond the southern line.

This was undoubtedly the scene Tuesday night, October 28, 2003. How was this possible?

Chapter Twelve
Battleground

There is no neutral ground in the universe: every square inch, every split second is claimed by God and counterclaimed by Satan.

C.S. LEWIS

Chapter Twelve
Battleground

IN THE SPRING of 2006, Frankie and Alex began driving down from Cuyamaca on Sunday mornings to come to church with us. Alex usually joined Danielle and Juliette in the children's ministry classrooms, while 19-year-old Frankie sat in the worship service with Joni and me. One Sunday, Frankie drove down without Alex.

Joni, Frankie and I sat in the middle section of the big gymnasium as the contemporary band began to play. The pastor and his wife sat at the end of our row, directly across from Joni. She watched the pastor reviewing his sermon notes, seemingly oblivious to everyone around him. His preparation was intense. He looked as if he were getting ready to go into battle, like one of those brave firefighters who suit up to face down a life-threatening firestorm.

And in fact, he was.

Evangelical pastors are, in essence, the beckoning carnival barkers of the eternal realm. They stand, megaphones in hand, in lanes of bumper to bumper spiritual traffic while multitudes of lost souls roll slowly by them toward their mysterious final destination. The evangelist has an unenviable task. His life's work is to convince these non-believing spiritual travelers that they are actually in great jeopardy — that though they may have removed both hands from the steering wheels of their eternal lives, a terrifying and flesh consuming destination awaits them all the same, just beyond the visible dimension. If the preacher succeeds enough to occasion actual fear, things *really* get difficult. Now the pastor's appeal must pivot them toward belief in a loving, rescuing, *invisible* God. A Holy Spirit who wants to save them from a hideous dwelling place full of sinister spirits (also invisible) who eagerly await freshly condemned human souls.

"This day I call heaven and earth as witnesses against you that I have set before you life and death, blessings and curses. Now choose life"

(Deut. 30:19)

These earthly sojourners must somehow be persuaded to abandon their hell bound vehicles, engines running, and begin trudging uphill on a narrow footpath in the opposite direction. Improbable seems too mild a word. Impossible is more like it. Is it any wonder that Christians are held in such contempt in the non-believing world?

Jesus explained: *"You can enter God's Kingdom only through the narrow gate. The highway to hell is broad, and its gate is wide for the many who choose that way But the gateway to life is very narrow and the road is difficult, and only a few ever find it."* (Mt 7:13-14) NLT... Then he went further and stated that: *"Yes, I am the gate. Those who come in through me will be saved. They will come and go freely and will find good pastures."*

(Jn 10:9) NLT

A Spirit-filled church service is akin to having a backstage pass behind the world's immense stage. But life isn't a play and there aren't any actors — we all get the leading role. Each life comes with a death scene at the end. You, playing the role of, *well,* you.

This verse of scripture from John's gospel describes it perfectly:

> *There was a man named Nicodemus who was one of the Pharisees and an important Jewish leader. One night Nicodemus came to Jesus and said, "Teacher, we know you are a teacher sent from God, because no one can do the miracles you do unless God is with him."*
>
> *Jesus answered, "I tell you the truth, unless you are born again, you cannot be in God's kingdom."*
>
> *Nicodemus said, "But if a person is already old, how can he be born again? He cannot enter his mother's womb again. So how can a person be born a second time?"*
>
> (John 3:1-4) NCV

When instantaneous spiritual redemption (to be born again) happens to a person, what transpires within the mind and heart of a human being to compel them to flip such an unlikely switch? Can anyone make so dramatic a change all by themselves? Who could make such a jump? It only follows that for such a personally supernatural experience to be possible, the Lord, himself, would need to be present wherever we are when we first believe.

> *Where can I go from your Spirit? Where can I flee from your presence? If I go up to the heavens, you are there; if I make my bed in the depths, you are there.*
>
> (Psalms 139: 7-8)

When the worship music ended, Joni, Frankie, and I took our seats. Pastor Mike climbed two steps up to the stage and settled behind the podium at the middle of it. He asked everyone to please turn in their Bibles to Luke 16:19. Pages rustled from every direction in the big gym.

"I *love* that sound," Pastor Mike said.

After the laughter died down, Pastor Mike became serious. He looked out and warned everyone that his sermon would not be a joyful one. He said he was going to preach on what he believed to be the most terrifying story Jesus ever told. Because Jesus used an actual name, biblical scholars believed it to be the true story of a rich man who actually lived, and an actual beggar named Lazarus.

THE BEGGAR AND THE RICH MAN

"The rich man wore fine clothes and lived in luxury every day," Pastor Mike began. "While Lazarus was covered with sores and longed for the scraps of food thrown out for the dogs from the rich man's table. The filthy dogs even licked the beggar's sores. The beggar died and the angels carried Lazarus to Abraham's side. The rich man also died and was buried after a great funeral with many mourners." Pastor Mike picked up his Bible and said he was going to read the rest of the story straight out of Luke's Gospel:

"In hell, where he was in torment, he looked up and saw Abraham far away, with Lazarus by his side. So he called to him, 'Father Abraham, have pity on me and send Lazarus to dip the tip of his finger in water and cool my tongue, because I am in agony in this fire.'

"But Abraham replied, 'Son, remember that in your lifetime you received your good things, while Lazarus received bad things, but now he is comforted here and you are in agony. And besides all this, between us and you a great chasm has been fixed, so that those who want to go from here to you cannot, nor can anyone cross over from there to us.'

"He answered,'Then I beg you, father, send Lazarus to my father's house, for I have five brothers. Let him warn them, so that they will not come to this place of torment.'

"Abraham replied, 'They have Moses and the Prophets; let them listen to them.'

'No, father Abraham,' he said, 'but if someone from the dead goes to them, they will repent.'

"He said to him, 'If they do not listen to Moses and the Prophets, they will not be convinced even if someone rises from the dead.'"

(Luke 16:24-31)

Frankie listened closely as Pastor Mike asked that we all consider the eternal agony of the rich man, and the eternal comfort of Lazarus, the beggar.

"One man was rich and the other was poor, but that had little to do with each man's everlasting destination. Our relationship with *God* is the only thing that matters," Pastor Mike stated.

The sermon brought to mind the strong experience I had the day *I* first believed, twenty-one years before. That was the day I realized I was not just a random hunk of flesh headed for a hole in the ground, but a spiritual being with an eternal destination. An awful one. I sat with my God-loving wife, Joni, in this same church, on January 6, 1985, and I raised my hand. I asked Jesus to save me, to make his home in me. Then He did. The Holy Spirit rushed into me like a blitzing outside linebacker. Christ's abounding love was too beautiful for me to contain. The man who until moments before had been a snarling cynic was now overflowing with tears of joy.

Frankie was having his *own* moment of conviction. He later would tell me it seemed like the preacher was speaking directly to him. What happened next pierced the young man's heart as sharply as a dagger. A moment of self-awareness like he could never have imagined flashed through his being. Dread flooded into Frankie's soul. The Holy Spirit revealed to his awakening spirit what existed right behind the world's curtain. The young man had a choice to make, and as is true of any decision made without coercion, there must be more than one possible outcome. In an instant, Frankie experienced utter clarity. It was a moment of reality and fearful confirmation. Frankie was shown what it was to be eternally separated from God.

Hell was real.

God's Spirit descended slowly until He was face to face with Frankie, just inches in front of him. The Spirit's magnificent light was good, *so* good that though Frankie could not see it, he could sense God's benevolent illumination all the same. In Frankie's moment of conviction he had admitted to himself and to the Lord that he was powerless to erase even *one* of his many offenses against God. He was dirty, and his own hands could never scrub himself clean. If Frankie was ever to be allowed into the Lord's sinless dwelling place, *God* was going to have to clean him up. Frankie didn't know much, but he knew enough to call upon the one true Savior.

"*Jesus! Help me!*"

Immediately, Frankie was overcome with great joy.

Pastor Mike concluded by preparing the believers for the Lord's supper. "Anyone who belongs to Jesus is welcome to participate," he said as the band behind him began to play.

I turned to Frankie. Tears of joy were streaming down his face. As the music continued, I leaned over and whispered a question into his ear: "Are you saying yes to Jesus, Frankie?" He nodded his head. "Yes?" I again asked the quiet young man.

The Lord had heard him loud and clear. He turned to face me and said firmly through unashamed tears. "Yes."

"Then come with me."

Joni and I were thrilled to share in Frankie's Spiritual baptism. We were overjoyed at being present at the Lord's acceptance of him into the kingdom of heaven. After church I shared the good news with Pastor Mike. I introduced Frankie to him.

The pastor engulfed him in a big hug. "Welcome to the family, Frankie! We're glad to have you!"

"In the same way, I tell you, there is rejoicing in the presence of the angels of God over one sinner who repents."

(Luke 15:10)

MARCH 2012

Over eight years have passed since the Cedar Fire blackened 127 square miles in the middle of San Diego County. Kathy, Frank, and their children still live in their home in the midst of the Cuyamaca Mountains. The trees of the once beautiful forest still stand together like thousands of weathered gray tombstones on steeply sloping graveyards. They are ghosts of the Cedar Fire.

Little Anna is a tall eighth grader now, and Alex, now also a born again believer, is 6' 3" and a high school senior. Frankie and Veronica have left the mountain to complete their studies at a distant university.

Chocolate, Veronica's comical chicken, lived a long life after miraculously surviving the Cedar Fire. Two of the Scalari's horses, Cindy and Elyse, are gone, sold when the economy plunged and the price of alfalfa doubled, but Neo and Skip still roam the pasture, wandering into the apple orchard for a snack now and then. Neo looks for Veronica every morning and evening at feeding time. Other hands feed him, touch him, and speak kind words to him, but Neo belongs to Veronica, the one who loved him at the moment he had lost everything, even the will to live.

As for the Stelleys, Danielle and Juliette are high schoolers, and both are good students. Joni and I remain forever grateful to the Lord for the grace, mercy, power and love He has showered upon us, and the miracles He has allowed us to be witness to. The road I have taken my family down while writing this book has been a difficult one. I once asked the Lord to put a hedge around my family. A supernatural barrier that the evil one would have to back away from. Soon that small quiet whisper returned.

"The hedge is already in place. God is protecting you."

I hadn't thought of that. As bad as the satanic realm's oppression had been, the evil spirits craved to do much worse to my family. God wouldn't let them.

I am amazed that the Lord gave me one of his earthly treasures to be my wife. Thank you, Joni, I love you more than I've ever been able to express. Thanks to Danielle and Juliette for loving their dad when I wasn't very lovable, which, if I'm honest, was too often during the four year process of bringing this story to life. I offer my heartfelt thanks to Frank, Kathy, and their children. This book would never have been possible without their generous help. But the story isn't over.

A while back, I sat in front of a blank page on my iMac asking the Lord to help me understand it all. I had spent years peeling back onion-like layers of supernatural implications that came with the Cedar Fire miracles. The more I thought about them, the more inconceivable they became. I couldn't focus the picture. I asked the Lord my questions...

Why Kathy and Frank's property, God? What were the miracles for? Why didn't the rest of the Scalari's come to believe in you? What more does it take?

His answer came in the form of a metaphor. What follows was simply given to me. I began filling page after page as if a starter pistol had been fired...

The truth is, in the end we *all* burn down. These bodies of ours end up looking like the forest did after the Cedar Fire—ugly, ruined, lifeless. All of our worldly possessions, all of our earthly pretensions, and all of our prideful accomplishments—*everything* is stripped from us when we die. Who will stand up to defend you on that day? Who will love you and take care of you then? Jesus. If you trusted him while you were alive.

Think about the man who started the Cedar Fire. He committed a single sin, like Adam did when he ate the forbidden fruit. He kindled a small flame, but it grew. It spread like, *well*, like wildfire. Once the fire-starter's sin, his match-sized flame, was released, there was no calling it back. Roaring flames burned down forests, they devoured homes, and they killed people. One man's small flame kindled the largest wildfire in the history of California.

Then the firefighters came and fought the firestorm with everything they had. Thousands of firemen from different places worked together to try to stop the fire. They saved people and homes from being burned, but the fire was too strong. Many people died. A few stubborn homeowners refused to leave. They had no idea about the power within the Cedar Fire's flames. They thought if they just worked hard enough they could save their homes all by themselves. The firemen warned them they might burn if they stayed put, that the fire was coming quickly, but some wouldn't listen.

There are two types of people who die in a firestorm. The victims who are caught unaware at the beginning of the fire, then, in the midst of it, the stubborn, prideful, self-determined people who refuse to believe that the wildfire has the power to kill them. They won't bow. Instead, they burn. Folks are like that about belief in the Lord, too. Most young people believe they're immortal. They think they're never going to die. When a young person dies, it's usually quick. Death comes unexpectedly, like it did for the Cedar Fire's bleary-eyed victims that first morning. Older folk's hearts become harder and harder toward God the longer they live. Nonbelievers become increasingly stubborn in their disbelief as the years pass, like the people who die at the end of a firestorm. They die with busy hands, working out their own path to salvation. They don't need *God* to save them from burning, they can do it themselves. When death comes for them, they're still struggling to control what cannot be controlled.

The firemen saved what they could, like the old gold mining town of Julian. Meanwhile, the nearby mountains burned to the ground. Cuyamaca truly was a magical place before the Cedar Fire. I've seen the locals weep over what happened to their forest. Yes, it was very beautiful, and yes, it's a shame what happened to it, but God has a lesson for us in its destruction. The Bible says someday each believer will stand before Jesus in heaven.

For we must all appear before the judgment seat of Christ, that each one may receive what is due him for the things done while in the body, whether good or bad.

(2Cor 5:10)

For no one can lay any foundation other than the one already laid, which is Jesus Christ. If any man builds on this foundation using gold, silver, costly stones, wood, hay or straw, his work will be shown for what it is, because the Day will bring it to light. It will be revealed with fire, and the fire will test the quality of each man's work. If what he has built survives, he will receive his reward. If it is burned up, he will suffer loss; he himself will be saved, but only as one escaping through the flames.

(1Cor 3:11-15)

Only the things we do in *His* name will remain forever. The junk I've done in my name, my sinful thoughts, my sinful acts, will be burned in front of me when I stand before Christ. I imagine it will be quite a bonfire. Every shameful act, every lustful thought or negative intention, every cuss word, every time I loved money more than God — I'm in for quite a show.

The Bible speaks to this directly:

> *But who can endure the day of his coming? Who can stand when he appears? For he will be like a refiner's fire or a launderer's soap. He will sit as a refiner or purifier of silver;*
>
> (Malachi 3:2-3)

When the judgment flames of my earthly works die down and go out, there'll be something left in the midst of the ashes. Everything I did for Jesus will have made it through my sinful bonfire. A small stack of treasure will be shining in the middle of the Refiner's fire. Many folks will see almost everything they ever did burn up in front of them, except for one thing: their trust in Christ. They will live in heaven forever.

We're all like the man who started that fire in a certain way. We have sinful matches in our hands, every one of us. We can set fire to our life, or to other people's lives if we want to, just like the man who kindled the Cedar Fire. It just takes one sinful, willful, striking of a match.

The miracles displayed during the Cedar Fire on the Scalari's ranch are an example of Christ's power to save — to save a house and a barn from terrible fire, to save every one of those apple trees too. Christ wants to save me, to save you, and anyone else who will call out in faith to him, from eternal separation from God's love. Jesus redeemed that property from consuming fire in an impossible way just like He'll redeem you! How is it that nothing burned on that entire property smack in the middle of a raging firestorm? Kathy and Frank's piece of land wasn't special before the fire. It didn't deserve saving anymore than the rest of the mountain. So, tell me, why didn't it burn?

It didn't burn because a mother and her young daughter prayed for that property to be protected in Jesus' name, for the Father's glory. In other words, so God's fame would spread among men. The Scalari property was redeemed out of the heat and flames of the Cedar Fire to honor God. It was a gift from Jesus to the Father.

These are the words of Christ himself:

"Believe me when I say that I am in the Father and the Father is in me; or at least believe on the evidence of the miracles themselves. I tell you the truth, anyone who has faith in me will do what I have been doing. He will do even greater things than these, because I am going to the Father. And I will do whatever you ask in my name, so that the Son may bring glory to the Father. You may ask me for anything in my name and I will do it."

(John 14:11-14)

What is your relationship with God like? You have taken this journey with me this far so we can safely say that you are at least curious about Him. Perhaps this testimony seems too good to be true. Maybe the loving, omnipresent, all-powerful God that I have described to you throughout this book is unknown within your personal experience. You have looked at my photographs and read my testimony, but something is missing. You need your *own* photographs, your *own* evidences of God's love for you affecting outcomes in *your* life. How will you acquire this supernatural evidence? I have a surprise for you. Chances are, you already have. Let me leave you with the story Frank astonished me with in early 2010.

I could say, 'The darkness will hide me. Let the light around me turn into night.' But even the darkness is not dark to you. The night is as light as the day; darkness and light are the same to you.

(Ps 139:11-12) NCV

It was a chilly Saturday when Joni, the girls and I drove up to the Cuyamaca's to spend the day with the Scalaris. Veronica and Frankie were home from college and everyone was in high spirits. It was too cold to be outside, so while the young folks were happily playing card games in the dining room, and Joni and Kathy were chatting in the kitchen, preparing the afternoon's dinner, Frank and I sat in leather chairs in the family room, regularly stoking the potbellied stove. We were having a wonderful time telling each other stories from our childhoods. He told me about growing up as an only child, how lonely he was, and he fondly remembered his Uncle Leo, the special man who had seen his potential and showed him the only real love he received as a boy.

Frank disappeared into the kitchen. He returned with a bottle of very expensive red wine and two glasses.

"I've been saving this for a special occasion," said Frank. He poured a glass for each of us and slumped back into his chair.

Sparks flew as I tossed another wedge into the stove. I clanked the grated door shut. Frank took a large slug of wine. Something was odd about him. He didn't look right.

"Something's bothering you."

Frank started to tell me something — then he stopped. He took another drink.

"C'mon, Doc. Level with me."

"You're going to think I'm crazy," he said.

"You probably think I'm crazy. It might even things up."

He took another sip. "Okay, but I'm warning you."

"Properly noted."

"I'm an only child, you know. I was seven, just a little kid, but I still think about it a lot. I even dream about it." Frank grabbed the wine bottle and offered it to me.

"No, I'm good."

He emptied it into his glass.

"My family lived in upstate New York. Syracuse. It was after midnight on a moonless midsummer evening in 1967..."

Little Frank was sound asleep in his downstairs bedroom in their drafty old two-story house. His mom and dad were upstairs, asleep

226

in their bedroom—miles away to a 7-year-old. Suddenly, the boy was jolted awake by the sound of breaking glass. Someone had broken into the basement directly below him. He could hear scuffling footsteps and vile drunken cursing coming from some really bad men.

"You were seven?" I asked. "You must've been terrified."

"I've never been so frightened in all my life. I sat up in bed petrified—*speechless* with fear. I could see a flash of light through a crack in the hardwood floor. I tried to call for my dad but no sound would come out. The men began screaming words I'd never heard before. I started to shake. I clutched my blanket to my face and I cried, Greg. I really cried."

"What were they after?" I asked.

"I don't know. They were drunk. Maybe they broke into the wrong basement but they were looking for something."

"Or someone?"

One of the intruders lit a match. Little Frank looked over the edge of his bed and saw flashes of flame through the crack in the floor. The boy screamed. The man with the match looked up. He laughed.

Little Frank thought: *They're going to get me! They're going to come up and get me!*

Frank told me how he had experienced an overwhelming feeling of dread, how he couldn't breathe, and how he had sat up on the edge of his bed and scrunched his eyes shut tight, not wanting to see. Finally, in desperation, with the bad men coming and little Frank all alone in the dark, he managed to speak three words...

"Please help me."

A few seconds later the boy felt a hand—a *man's* hand on his shoulder.

Frank and I downed the last of the wine in our glasses. It sure didn't sound like this story had a happy ending. My thoughts were full of ominous scenarios. *At least he's finally telling someone about it—that's the important thing. Whatever happened to him that night, it's better that he get it out in the open.*

I studied Frank's face. He wasn't mournful. He wasn't angry either. I saw my scientist friend beginning to choke up. Whatever he was about to tell me had marked him. He couldn't let it go. I felt my own tears beginning to well up. Frank continued...

"I could feel *fingers* — a man's warm reassuring fingers. He gave my shoulder a gentle squeeze... My shivering stopped. I took a deep breath. Somehow, all my fear had vanished. Somehow, I knew the bad men had fled. I was told, without words, that everything would be all right."

The hand remained on 7-year-old Frank as he sat there in the dark. And his heart was filled to overflowing with an intense *love*. Frank confessed how no one before or since had ever shown him that kind of overwhelming love. He had sat there smiling from ear to ear. Little Frank got out of bed, felt his way over to the light switch and flipped it on. The door was shut tight. He scanned his room. His maple-framed bed still stood in the corner near the window. His plastic dinosaurs still lay strewn across the braided rug. The young boy checked the closet and looked under the bed, but no one was there.

As we sat before the potbellied stove I asked Frank who it was that had rescued him that night. Who could have removed his petrifying fear in an instant and replaced it with such a powerful love? Who could have slipped into his room without making a sound? Who could have touched his shoulder and not caused him to have a heart attack? *Who?* It was an incredible story and the one question that screamed out was — who had been there to protect little Frank?

Frank told me he didn't know. That was all. He just didn't know. I wasn't surprised, but I learned a profound truth about all the Franks of the world that day.

The lesson is this: God hasn't given up on you.

The Lord had preserved Frank time after time during his life, seeking him out, watching over him, showing love to him, even displaying His limitless power to him during the Cedar Fire. God knew Frank long before he rescued him in his bed that night so long ago. He would love him until his last breath on earth. Then, finally, Jesus would give Frank what he wanted.

The question remained. What did Frank want?

"I am the resurrection and the life. He who believes in me will live, even though he dies; and whoever lives and believes in me will never die. Do you believe this?"

(John 11:25)

GOD
INSIDE THE FIRE

An Amazing True Story

GREG STELLEY

Danielle,Joni,Greg,Juliette

ACKNOWLEDGMENTS

When I began work on this project four years ago, I had no idea how to write a book. I had one sharp tool in my writer's toolbox. I could describe with words what I saw in my mind. That wasn't nearly enough, but I realized if *I* didn't write this story it would never be written. So, as Stephen King accurately describes in "ON WRITING" (his nonfiction memoir which I nearly committed to memory), I pushed off from the dock, sat down in my rowboat and began rowing across the Pacific. Many people helped me along the way, baling water through those first drafts to keep me afloat. My grateful thanks to my readers:

Jane Parker, who baled water before anyone else and forced me to pick a tense and stay with it.

Professor Festus Ndeh, my dear friend, and a fierce advocate of compound sentences.

Eugenia Ndeh, who loved the story and encouraged me at a crucial time.

Ila Mason edited and contributed a good line here and there.

Twila, Cheryl, and Donna gave me insight into what worked and what didn't. Thanks to all of you for your opinions.

Thanks to Danielle for her red pen questions in the margin, and thanks to Juliette for being my *Goofy Grape*.

Susan Rohrer encouraged and corrected me. I needed both.

Sandra Holcome steered me away from the rocks.

Much appreciation to Scott Morris for his talent and insight. Scott helped bring this story to life and made me a better writer.

Many thanks to Jason Kasperski for several helpful draft evaluations.

I owe a great debt of gratitude to my literary agent, Judy Hilsinger, at Heartfelt Books and Films: You believed me, and you trusted God from the first time I told you this impossible story. Neither one of us could let it go.

Thanks to Frank, Kathy, Frankie, Veronica, Alex and Anna for their generosity with the details, and for allowing me to tell this story honestly.

Much love to my wife, Joni. All of this is because of you, sweetie. Thanks for sticking with me through the darkness. I found the Light.

Made in the USA
Lexington, KY
04 November 2013